THE REFRACTIVE THINKER®

AN ANTHOLOGY OF DOCTORAL WRITERS

VOLUME XIII

Entrepreneurship

Growing the Future of Business

Edited by **Dr. Cheryl A. Lentz**

THE REFRACTIVE THINKER® PRESS

The Refractive Thinker®: An Anthology of Higher Learning
Vol XIII: Entrepreneurship: Growing the Future of Business

The Refractive Thinker® Press
www.RefractiveThinker.com
blog: www.DissertationPublishing.com

Please visit us on Facebook and like our Fan page.
www.facebook.com/refractivethinker

Books are available through The Refractive Thinker® Press at special discounts for bulk purchases for the purpose of sales promotion, seminar attendance, or educational purposes. Special volumes can be created for specific purposes and to organizational specifications. Please contact us for further details.

Copyright © 2017 by The Refractive Thinker® Press
Managing Editor: Dr. Cheryl A. Lentz • DrCherylLentz@gmail.com

Library of Congress Control Number: 2013945437

Volume ISBNs   Soft Cover   978-0-9974399-5-3
                 E-book/PDF   978-0-9974399-6-0
                 *Kindle and electronic versions available

Refractive Thinker® logo by Joey Root; The Refractive Thinker® Press logo design by Jacqueline Teng; cover design and production by Gary A. Rosenberg.

Printed in the United States of America

10 9 8 7 6 5 4 3 2 1

Contents

The important thing is not to stop questioning.
Curiosity has its own reason for existing. One cannot
help but be in awe when he / she contemplates the
mysteries of eternity, of life, of the marvelous
structure of reality. It is enough if one tries merely
to comprehend a little of this mystery every day.
Never lose a holy curiosity.

—ALBERT EINSTEIN

Foreword

I'm honored and a bit astonished to be writing the foreword for such a prestigious academic publication as *The Refractive Thinker®*. I'll share a little secret. The bane of my existence is that I have no formal education; no college, no university, no alma mater. There are many things hanging on the wall in my office, but a college diploma isn't one of them.

It was clear from my kindergarten report cards that I was a smart child, but I had a fairly bad case of the wiggles. I just couldn't sit still for too long; my teachers said my attention span was short. Today, they call it Attention Deficit Disorder (ADD). In my opinion, I had no deficit; they just had me on too much sugar that sitting still was just impossible!

I must have been vaccinated with a phonograph needle, because I was also quite the little chatterbox. This skill came in rather handy however; when this vivacious and outgoing 5-year-old was cast as Mary Poppins in the Christmas play! I remembered every line I was to recite and every word to every song I belted out so proudly! That was it! My very first captive audience! *I was hooked!* The stage was definitely in my future. Today I'm a sugar-free pre-diabetic, still wiggle a lot, and my attention span is shorter than ever! At 59 years of age, my memory isn't as good either.

Lesson #1: The classroom life isn't for everyone, sugar is bad for you, and you can pull just about anything out of a supercalifragilisticexpialidocious handbag! Keep one close by as you go through life! You never know what you may come in handy.

I knew from a very young age I wanted to be rich and famous. Watching movie legends Rita Hayworth and Ava Gardner dance and sing their way across the silver screen in front of millions of adoring fans, it was clear to me that I wanted to become a member of *that* club. Alas, Mother Nature had other plans! My buckteeth, flat chest, protruding ears and gangly long legs left me little hope. *Oh, woe was 12-year-old me!* Time, thank goodness, would become my friend. I grew into womanhood more graciously and elegantly. With a little help from a dental retainer in my early teens, everything else worked itself out.

Lesson #2: Be patient with you as you grow *into* yourself. Keep your dream as a very clear vision at all times.

Nothing was going to stop me from the bright lights and the big cities! New York City was the first stop in the early 1980s before finding a modeling agent in Paris. At 18, I was going to be an international model in the French fashion magazines and on the designer runways. Off I went to Europe. With a slow start, I did a few jobs, got horribly homesick (no Internet or Skype in those days; an airmailed letter took two weeks to get back and forth to family!), and I just didn't think I was good enough. The other girls seemed so much better than me . . . somehow, they were so much prettier. As I got close to my dreams; everything imploded. I asked the question: was this life what I *really* wanted? I got on a plane and went back home.

Lesson #3: Pack some sunglasses for those bright lights as they may glare in a way you weren't expecting. Self-doubt and comparing yourself to others is wasted energy. You are good enough . . . *enough said!* No need to be impulsive . . . airfare to and from Europe is very expensive. Think things over carefully before boarding a plane back home! If at first you don't succeed, try again, and **don't look back, because you're not going in that direction.**

A year later, I ventured out again only this time to Italy. With a new agent, not as fearful, and lots of hard work, my career became that of a supermodel. I walked the runways in my dreams; Milan, Rome, Paris, New York, London, Tokyo, and more. I obtained many beauty contracts and magazine covers. I began working on Italian television variety shows and acting in movies. *Dreams do come true.* Please forgive me for a moment if I seem a bit braggadocio, but I never had a modeling lesson, acting lesson, singing lesson or hosting lesson before. I brought to the forefront my strengths or what they call *God-given talent.* I was a natural.

Lesson #4: Start with the talents you were given . . . lead with your strengths. Be fearless; your fear serves no one. If it's what you *really* want, you will find a way, find the money, find the courage, and find yourself. The latter is priceless. I never really thought someone had to *find* themselves. Perhaps at times throughout their life they were merely temporarily *misplaced.* The road to self-discovery is long sometimes and for some it never ends.

Anxious to move into television production, I opened my company in Rome and started producing shows for Italian television, the Miss Universe pageant chief among them. A 3-hour live broadcast in prime time; every producers dream! Admittedly, this event was a risky venture, as I had never taken a class on media production either or any class that might have assisted in my entrepreneurial efforts. To the outside world, my work was a triumph. I won't say that this was my undoing, but the company grew far too quickly for my own good, getting away from me; my bank account suffered greatly for it.

Lesson #5: Stick to what you know until you know what you need to know to move forward. Cover every base and make sure to have a good lawyer that oversees your every move moving forward. Take the classes, read the books, and prepare for the unexpected. Success is simply where opportunity and preparedness meet.

Although my successes are many, my **un**-successes are many as well. I simply never use the word failure. If you tried and didn't succeed, the success is in the trying. It's in the risk you take, but it's **never** a failure.

Lesson #6: Pick yourself up, dust yourself off, and never give in to failure. There were many times I was too down to look up, too scared to take the next step; completely devoid of ideas and creativity, and more times than I care to remember, downright depressed. I knew that staying in this condition didn't move me closer to my new goals, and I hated the feeling. This feeling simply didn't serve me.

Fast-forward 20 years, now in my mid-fifties. Once I left Europe 13 years ago to move back to the United States, I had to start all over again, only this time without the supermodel face and body. Don't' get me wrong, I didn't want to be a supermodel for life. It was the normal progression of things that I would age and must face Mother Nature. But, the world is my stage, remember? Life is my classroom.

Now what? What was the next step?

Technology created new processes at the speed of light and I was way behind the eight ball. My time and resources went into traveling to events, networking, courses and classes. It wasn't yet clear what I would do moving forward, but I was steadfast in creating a new dream.

So here it is . . . I created my signature beauty and lifestyle brand for women. I will be offering products that help women look good, feel good, be good, and live a greater good—the four pillars of self-esteem.

The good news? Life begins at fifty. Everything before was just a dress rehearsal!

So, while I don't have a diploma hanging in my office, I have been educated on the streets of the world. I've been taught by every person that lied to me, cheated on me, stole from me, defrauded me, kicked me when I was down and spit in my face. I've been taught by every jealous woman who had not come in to her own power and formed by every mean girl and vicious clique. AND I'm still here. This, by the way, is main reason I have created EnvelopHer. com—the Multi-Media platform for women, EnvelopHer app, and EnvelopHer events. This is a safe place where women encounter, engage and encourage one another globally. Here women who beat from the heart are inspired to rise into living their greater good. *No mean girls need apply.*

Ultimately, the question to ask yourself is: am I where I want to be? If not, change it. Look at ALL the tools you have in your toolbox. What have you learned along your journey (both in and out of the classroom) and how will you share your gifts with the world? Remember, the premise of this award-winning series is how do you live your life as a refractive thinker? How do you live your life beyond the box, always reinventing yourself, embracing failure, and embracing life's lessons wherever they may come from? Embrace the heart of the entrepreneur to create *your* world, to live *your* life, on *your* terms. Never settle for anything less than everything. Dare to dream big. Dare to change the world. No one benefits by you playing small. If I can do it, so can you; your world stage is waiting.

Clarissa Burt
www.ClarissaBurt.com
www.EnvelopHer.com

About the Author . . .

 Entrepreneur, television / video producer, public speaker, author, writer, award-winning actress and emcee has all the makings of a best-selling novel. At 18, Clarissa was a top model with the Wilhelmina Modeling Agency in Manhattan. Soon after she moved to Milan and quickly began appearing on over a 100 magazine covers such as Harper's Bazaar, Vogue, and Cosmopolitan as well as on most of the major runway shows in Milan, Rome, Paris, New York, and Japan. This led to work for cosmetic houses Revlon, Dior, and Carita', Helena Rubenstein and her selection as the worldwide "Face" for Orlane Cosmetics.

Clarissa has performed in over 20 movies and can be remembered in award winning films such as Warner Brother's *The Never Ending Story, part II,* where she played the Mean Queen *Xayide* and as Giulia in the Italian production *Caruso Pascosky di Padre Polacco.*

This Who's Who of International and American Women added television producer to her credits in 1999. Clarissa Burt Media Group founded in Italy began with productions that included the nationally broadcast three-hour live broadcast of the Miss Universe Pageant, *The World Sports Awards, Quizzauto, and Behind the Scenes with The Miss;* all garnering her various coveted media awards internationally. Moving into radio production, *Clarissa Burt Talks* featured this multi-talented media celebrity on Voice America and World Talk Radio where she interviewed knowledgeable entrepreneurs and prominent thought leaders.

Clarissa has been the Beauty Editor for such international publications as *The LA Fashion Magazine, Fashion Faces, Runway,* and *Woman and Bride.* One can find her articles also in *The Huffington Post, Supermodels Unlimited, Bella Petite, Discover Phoenix,* and *Today's Innovative Woman* to name a few. In 2012-13, Ms. Burt also co-authored the best sellers *The Rise, Off the Coast of Zanzibar,* and *Stickability* with Greg S. Reid and was featured in the book *Women without Barriers* by Dolores Seright. Sharon Lechter highlighted Clarissa in her 2014 release *Think and Grow Rich for Women.*

An advocate for women's issues and leader of social change, this Who's Who of International and American Women recently launched *T.E.N. The Envelopment Network* Media for Women *EnvelopHer.com* an online multimedia portal, where women *Encounter, Engage and Encourage* providing educative, entertaining and empowering content. *The EnvelopHer.com* website offers content pertinent to women's issues through video interviews, articles, a magazine, blog, articles and a radio show.

Clarissa is also the first American to present at the Kremlin and be on the front page of a Russian newspaper. Clarissa's extensive international social work garnered her two private audiences with Pope John Paul II. As a women's advocate and a leader of social change for a new standard of living Clarissa was instrumental as *Ambassador to the United States for the Walking Africa campaign* that awarded African Women the Nobel Peace Prize in 2011.

Currently, Clarissa has launched her personal brand on QVC in Europe where she brings her sense of elegance and style to 'Made in Italy' products. Starting with a women's loungewear line, from her very first show, Clarissa boasts sold-out numbers.

Reprinted with permission from http://clarissaburt.com/clarissa-burt-bio/

Preface

Welcome to the award winning Refractive Thinker® Doctoral Anthology Series. We are thrilled to have you join us for the 15th volume in the series (Vol II was published 3 times), *Vol. XIII: Entrepreneurship: Growing the Future of Business*. Join us as we continue to celebrate the accomplishments of doctoral scholars from around the globe.

Our mission continues to be to get research off the coffee table, out of the Ivory Tower of academia, and into the hands of people who cannot only use, but also benefit from the many insights and wisdom found from doctoral research results. The goal is to continue to bridge the gap from the halls of academia into the halls of the business world. *The Refractive Thinker®* series continues to offer a resource by the many contributing doctoral scholars as they offer their chapter summaries of doctoral research well beyond the boundaries of a traditional textbook. Instead, the goal for this series is to use refractive thinking strategies to push the boundaries beyond conventional wisdom and to explore the paths not yet traveled particularly in this evolving digital age of technology.

As we bring 2017 to a close, this peer-reviewed publication offers readers insights and solutions to various challenges regarding entrepreneurs and entrepreneurship regarding the future of business, such as factors affecting Millennials, the relationship between hardiness and entrepreneurship, the importance of the clarity of business purpose, resilience relevance, conquering the myths of the easy entrepreneur, unethical business behavior, the lost tribe of the intrapreneur, the journey of experience of an entrepreneur, and the effectiveness of teaching entrepreneurship programs in higher education. Our hope is for you to find answers regarding effective strategies regarding the unique challenges of the entrepreneur to help guide your efforts in the boardroom, as well as the work space as part of this special edition *Vol XIII: Entrepreneurship: Growing the Future of Business* that have come from the research and pens of professional academicians and scholars around the world. The premise is to think not only *outside the box,* but also *beyond the box,* to create new solutions, to ask new questions, to proceed forward on new roads not yet explored or traveled. Our premise is to review academic research in a simple to digest executive summary format to offer new ways for business leaders to think about effective practices for strategies in their business based on what new research has to offer specifically growing the future of business.

With this volume, we add a new dimension to the series where Dr. Cheryl Lentz, *The Academic Entrepreneur* will conclude each chapter from a business point of view to link this doctoral research to applications for your business.

Remember, not only does *The Refractive Thinker®* series offer a physical book, we offer eBooks (Kindle, Nook, and Adobe eReader), and eChapters (individual chapters by author) that highlight the writings of your favorite Refractive Thinker® scholars, available through our website: http://www.RefractiveThinker. com, as well as www.Amazon.com . Be sure to also visit our social media to include our Facebook page, Twitter, our YouTube Channel, and our groups on LinkedIN® for further discussions regarding the many ideas presented here.

We look forward to your continued support and interest of the more than 130 scholars within *the Refractive Thinker®* doctoral community who contributed to this multi award winning anthology series from around the globe. Our mission that began with Volume 1 many years ago is to bring research out of academia for application in the world of business to provide answers to the many questions asked.

Acknowledgments

The foundation of scholarly research embraces the art of asking questions—to validate and affirm, what we do, and why. Through asking the right questions, the right answers are found. Leaders often challenge the status quo, to offer alternatives and new directions, to dare to try something bold and audacious, to try something that has never been tried before. This 15th publication of our beloved 15-time award winning *Refractive Thinker®* series required the continued belief in this new publishing model, of a peer-reviewed doctoral anthology, by those willing to continue forward on this voyage.

We are grateful for the help of many who made this collaboration possible. First, let me offer a special thank you to our **Peer Review Board,** to include Dr. Tracy Celaya, Dr. Ron Jones, Dr. Elmer Hall, and myself; and our **Board of Advisors** to include: Brian Jud, Dr. Les Paull, and Dr. Jody Sandwisch.

My gratitude extends with a well-deserved thank you to our production team: Gary Rosenberg (production specialist) and Joey Root, designer of the original Refractive Thinker® logo.

Thank you—we appreciate everyone's contributions to this scholarly collaboration.

Job well done!

My best to our continued success!

Dr. Cheryl Lentz
Managing Editor and Chief Refractive Thinker®

CHAPTER 1

Millennials: Disparity of Work Needs as an Entrepreneur

Dr. Judy Blando, Dr. Gayle Grant, Dr. D.Marie Hanson, Dr. Denise Land, & Dr. Huong Ly

Generational theorists postulate early life experiences can shape generational cohort members' worldviews and behaviors (Gardiner, Grace, & King, 2014). Inglehart (1977) authored the generational theory with a fundamental principle that maintains individuals born in the same period share common experiences and influences. Inglehart's principle is indicative of behaviors that appear consistent across members of the same generational group (Gardiner et al., 2014). The second principle of the generational theory maintains individuals also display generationally based differences in their work attitudes stemming from common influences (Kolbe, 2014). Disparity exists regarding how Millennials prefer to work regarding internal needs within the workplace and how this contradiction could adversely affect their success if Millennials become entrepreneurs.

Leadership defines culture (House et al., 1999). Accordingly, culture defines worldview, and worldview defines an individual. Friedman (1995) included parents (or caregivers) as leaders participatory in defining culture. The outcome may result in a Millennial sub-culture, worldview, and unique individual set who are ill-prepared to succeed in the contrasting Boomer worldview; however, the contrasting worldview of the Millennial entrepreneur could transcend that of the Boomer. Boomer entrepreneurs lean toward carefully constructed business plans that in the 22nd century volatile world of constant changes, often lends itself to failure in the first 5 years. Business plans built on causal thinking begin with a goal and charts the means to reach the goal. Causal thinking is the traditional adage of, "If I can predict the future, I can control it."

Sarasvathy (2001) developed the theory of effectuation; generally defined, effectuation is a form of reasoning that recognizes the future is primarily unpredictable, but is controlled by taking action. Saravathy's effectuation theory has its base in refractive thinking. Millennials lean toward refractive thinking: Instead of asking why, millennials ask *why not* or *what if* or *what's next*. Basing a business plan focused on preventing what could go wrong does not interest the Millennial. Possibilities are more interesting to this generation with a focus on the tomorrow.

Effectual or refractive thinkers start with what they must work with and look for new or different outcomes. Successful entrepreneurs, according to Sarasvathy's (2001) findings of more than 27 serial entrepreneurs, follow the adage of "If I can control the future, I do not need to predict it." Perhaps, the refractive thinking of a Millennial entrepreneur is most evident in their ability to bounce back, morph an idea, and start again following a different thread. Technological skills lend the Millennial a better grasp of website refinement and update, communication, and networking to get the needs of their businesses met; which is also from technology, as well as using what they have learned and starting from their refractive thinking.

As of 2017, often in the United States, four generations of employees interact together to collaborate to create a useful product or service. Within that group of employees is a generation representing the youngest of this labor force known as Generation Y or the Millennial generation, born between the years of 1977-1994 (U.S. Census Bureau, 2015). This group, while most recently out of college, joins the workforce with some unique personality traits, characteristics, attributes, views, and needs to be productive within that workplace. More than two-thirds of this millennial group often express a desire for workplace freedom; therefore, they are particularly enamored with the idea of entrepreneurship (Buzz Marketing Group, 2011). Entrepreneurship is often seen (or at least understood by this Millennial generation) as having more workplace freedom regarding greater creativity, manner of workplace behavior, workplace dress, hours / work schedule, work-life balance, and lack of micromanagement (Buzz Marketing Group, 2011; Martin, 2017).

As employees in the traditional workplace, the Millennials have many unique needs, which are perhaps *requirements* to maintain productivity that runs directly counter to the behaviors and traits needed by a successful entrepreneur. The Millennials, while at least outwardly expressing traits and desires they think would lead them to an entrepreneurial lifestyle and career, could prove problematic, as based on the actual workplace behaviors exhibited by this generation, which do not match the traits and behaviors of a successful entrepreneur (Khor & Mapunda, 2014). This misalignment is caused by an inaccurate assessment or unrealistic expectations of what it takes to be a successful entrepreneur. This inaccurate assessment of entrepreneurship could cause disappointment to the Millennial generation and wasted time and resources exploring avenues of employment that do not align well with actual behaviors, traits, and emotional workplace needs of this generation.

While Millennials often express a desire to be entrepreneurs (Giannantonio, & Hurly-Hansen, 2016), their workplace behavior exhibits needs counter to actions necessary in an entrepreneurial environment. Millennials often state the need to not be micromanaged, yet require high levels of constant, positive feedback, noting a need for a motivational boss in the workplace; which runs counter to an extreme lack of feedback in entrepreneurship where there is often no leader offering encouragement or motivation (Hall et al.,

2016). Millennials state a need for work / life balance, yet the life of an entrepreneur can be rigorous, taxing and without life work balance (D'Inino et al., 2007). Millennials note they want close relationships with their leaders, yet as entrepreneurs they would often be their own leader and have little to no contact with others in a number of work situations. Millennials need extreme levels of direction, instructions, and positive feedback, yet as entrepreneurs many times there is little to no feedback (Hall et al., 2016), and the only source of 'feedback' can be harsh and reality based, coming from their personal business losses (Giannantonio & Hurley-Hansen, 2016; Khor et al., 2014). Millennials want success quickly and with substantial financial rewards, yet the life of an entrepreneur is often challenged with delayed gratification, putting personal finances at risk and not reaping significant financial rewards for an extended period, sometimes even paying others before they pay themselves (Ng et al., 2010). Disparity exists in what Millennials crave as workers versus what they think they would have as entrepreneurs. This disparity regarding cognitive dissonance can be disappointing to an aspiring entrepreneurial Millennial, and perhaps detrimental economically to those investing in an entrepreneurial business.

Background

Many Millennials prefer the idea of entrepreneurship regarding long-term career goals (Buzz Marketing Group, 2011). The workplace characteristics of this group of Millennials appear to be at odds with the actual traits of a successful entrepreneur (Khor & Mapunda, 2014; Kilber, Barclay, & Ohmer, 2014). The internal needs of the Millennials versus the reality of a successful entrepreneur might be problematic from a financial sustainability aspect of entrepreneurship of those *want-to-be* Millennial business owners.

Outcomes from a U.S. national sample show the average

employee between the ages of 25 and 34 stayed with an organization 2.9 years from 2006 to 2016 (U.S. Department of Labor, 2016). Leaders struggle with the difficulty to attract and retain Millennial generation employees (Perkins, 2014). Many employers struggle with the Millennial generation workforce, seemingly affecting job satisfaction, motivation, and performance (Hsieh, 2016). According to Bursch and Kelly (2014), stereotypes associated with Millennials include having limited organization commitment and organization loyalty because of multiple organization and career changes. Additionally, Millennials are thought to require individualized recognition and feedback from the impression focused parenting had on their upbringing (Bursch & Kelly, 2014).

The traits of a successful entrepreneur include being a self-starter and the ability to function alone, at least at first, with little to no positive reinforcement (Zarbakhsh, Porhassani, Rahmani, Rad, & Poor, 2015). The entrepreneur is self-reliant, can work independently for long hours and can work without much direction, feedback, structure, or affirmation. Entrepreneurs often state they are not good at work / life balance because of their hours and lack of personal time (Kilber et al., 2014). A successful entrepreneur charts his or her own course and has the strength to follow out a vision with little to no encouragement or support, and the ability to stay self-motivated and believe in their product or service even if no one else does A successful entrepreneur charts his or her own course and has the strength to follow out a vision with little to no encouragement or support. The successful entrepreneur can exist via delayed gratification regarding position, business success and at times, even money earned (Dwyer, 2009; Rezai & Rahsepar, 2009).

Many entrepreneurial traits run counter to what Millennials stated they require from their traditional workplace and their employer (Dwyer, 2009; Rezai & Rahsepar, 2009). This contradiction leads to the question of how Millennials seeking self-employment and entrepreneurship would fair given their internal needs for such intensive and continued support within the traditional workplace. These Millennial requirements are the need for constant and speedy daily feedback. Millennials stated a need and insistence upon work-life balance (Hill, 2002). Millennials prefer detailed directions and close / open communications with their employer (Ferri-Reed, 2012). Millennials find the desire and even the need for open dialogs with their employer to be motivating, inspiring, affirming, and regularly delivered (Hall, 2016). The Millennials state they want a close relationship with their employer with regular feedback, yet this group is enamored with the idea and ideals of entrepreneurship. More than two-thirds of this generation state they aspire to entrepreneurship (Buzz Marketing Group, 2011), which in many if not most cases do not provide those internal reassurances and predictable, affirming, and comforting work environment. With entrepreneurship challenging in and of itself (Khor & Mapunda, 2014), one would have to wonder how or if these Millennials would fare as entrepreneurs.

Problem and Purpose

Millennials have unique personality traits, characteristics, and attributes regarding how they prefer to work (Giannantonio, & Hurley-Hansen, 2016). Whereas many Millennials appear to favor the idea of entrepreneurship, they have certain personality characteristics, needs, and *challenges* that could prevent them from becoming successful as entrepreneurs. The general business problem is that disparity exists regarding how Millennials prefer to work regarding internal needs within the workplace and how this contradiction could adversely affect their success if Millennials become entrepreneurs. The purpose of this chapter is to highlight methods millennials can use to become successful entrepreneurs.

Professional and Academic Literature

Generation Breakdown

The later part of the 20th century changed the way individuals view work (Ozkan & Solmaz, 2015). Work was viewed as the center of one's life; however, with improving technology expectations, the professional life was morphed. With different views of the professional life, the concept of generation became more prominent individuals began to study each generation more closely. *Generation* is a term used to define a group that shares important events at the same birth year and consume similar viewpoints affected by their environment and values. In the United States, there are distinct generations in the workplace. Each generation has likes, dislikes, characteristics, and expectations (Hammill, 2005). The perceptions of the work values of the three generations, Baby Boomer, Generation X, and Generation Y, are influenced by their historic, economic, social, and cultural experience (Angeline, 2011). With these different influential factors, tensions could occur between the groups if one group does not embrace the viewpoints of the other groups causing organizational chaos.

The Depression Era

Depression Era members were born from 1912 to 1921 and would be in the age range of 96 to 105 in 2017, are declining rapidly and are more than likely not to be in the 2017 workforce. (Hamilton, 2014). Depression-era individuals tend to be conservative, compulsive savers, and feel responsible to leave a legacy (Hamilton, 2014). Depression-era Americans are patriotic; their faith in the United States and its guiding institutions prepared them for the challenges of a double-dip recession and World War II. They had life worse, but stayed optimistic and expected all would be better (Allen, 2010).

World War II

The World War II generation, born before 1945 (this includes the Silent generation) is age 82 or older. The World War II generation also remains on the decline. The World War II generation has experience, knowledge, dedication, focus, stability, loyalty, emotional maturity, and perseverance (Dennis, 2008). This generation embraces the community mindset with less emphasis on *me* compared to Generation X.

The Baby Boomers

The term *Baby Boomers* refers to a group of individuals born during and post-World War II (Kaifi, Nafei, Khanfar, & Kaifi, 2012). Baby Boomers are the demographic group born during the post–World War II baby boom, approximately between the years 1946 and 1964 which would include people who are between 53 and 71 years old in 2017. Baby Boomers grew up in prosperous economic times and often are optimistic that the world continues to progress post-Depression Era. Some characteristic traits of this generation include (a) having time to enjoy their own hobbies, (b) believing in work-life balance, and (c) preferring to work remotely (Kaifi et al., 2012). Characteristics of this generation described by Angeline (2011) include diligent, focused, dedicated, loyal, self-motivated, thrifty, and value job security. Millennials are outnumbering the Baby Boomer generation (U.S. Census Bureau, 2015) and will replace the Baby Boomers as they retire. Boomers II or Generation Jones overlap the end of the Baby Boomer and beginning of the Generation X periods (Wellner, 2000). The individuals born near the beginning or end of a generation do not necessarily resemble those born in the middle. Individuals born in these cusps might identify with both generations (Zemke, Raines, & Filipczak, 2000).

Generation X

There are 44 to 50 million Americans in existence known as Generation X (Kaifi et al., 2012). These individuals were born between 1965 and 1980. This generation values work-life balance and focused on outcomes rather than processes (Heerwagen, Kelly, & Kampschroer, 2016). As managers, they allow their staff to have autonomy and rely on their technological proficiencies to achieve results. Characteristics of this generation are idealistic, individualistic, materialistic, skeptic, pro work-life balance, mobile, and value prompt recognition and reward (Angeline, 2011).

Millennials

The Millennial generation, or Generation Y, is the generation of children born between 1977 and 1994 and many have already entered college and the workforce. Compared to the other generations, somewhat surprisingly, the millennials share the most similarities with the Silent Generation. Millennials also experienced a major financial crisis during their formative years encouraging them to be financially conservative. Millennials are more likely to keep a larger amount of cash on hand than other generations (Bovino, 2015). Millennials are technologically savvy, which gives them more advantage with the changing work landscape. As the world adapted to the technological advancements, these individuals provide companies with skills not seen in previous generations (Kaifi et al., 2012).

Generation Y grew up in the digital age and has a competitive advantage with their technological skills. Millennials are averse to long-term commitments because of their experience with a high rate of divorces and layoffs of their parents (Kaifi et al., 2012). They crave flexibility in their careers and want to work in teams to achieve results rather than working individually. In addition, Angeline (2011) noted that these individuals are team players, willing to learn, adaptable to new technologies, and their philosophy is to live first, work later. Intrinsic motivation, such as activities that are pleasurable or things they consider fun is significantly higher for Generation Y than Generation X, Baby Boomers, and the cusp between Baby Boomer and Generation X (Leonard, Beauvais, & Scholl, 1999). Intrinsic process was also significantly higher for Generation X than Baby Boomers and the cusp between Baby Boomer and Generation X (Leavitt, 2014).

Millennials are a dynamic force beginning to emerge as leaders. Millennials are already accepting leadership roles. This dynamic population demands accountability, transparency, and change (Emeagwali, 2011). How millennials will be remembered by history is not yet clear. As the Baby Boomer generation retires, the next two generations will be planning, organizing, leading, and controlling the workforce. Millennials may have a competitive advantage because of their computer proficiencies. Bott, Faulk, Guntupalli, Devaraj, and Holmes (2011) concluded that Millennials are more engaged in the newer media, suggesting that "new media will become even more integrated into work processes" (p. 98); leaders should prepare accordingly for the millennial generation.

Generations Z and Alpha

Although employers are hard to understand and appreciate Generation Y workers, Generation Z employees are the next generation to consider. Generation Z includes individuals born after 2000 (Ozkan & Solmaz, 2015). This generation will penetrate the workforce soon, and their mindsets are different from their predecessors. They grew up with the Internet, mp3 players, social media, cell phones, PDAs, YouTube, and iPads. These individuals are happy, self-confident, and thrive on team spirit. Generation Z workers are the future. In 2015, they comprised about 7% of the workforce, but by 2019 almost 30 million will be employed (Charney, 2015). The contribution of this generation to the workforce is to be determined later because this group is barely entering the workforce. Whereas millennials likely do not hold important positions in the workforce yet, they should be groomed to take on those roles in the future (Jacoby, 2015). Generation Alpha, on the heels of Generation Z, begins with those born in 2010 or sooner. More than 2.5 million Generation Alphas are born globally every week. The Millennial population will be almost two billion when all are born (~2025). They started school in 2016 and will be the most formally educated generation, the most technology supplied generation, and globally the wealthiest generation ever (Williams, 2015).

Ethics

The Millennial generation is coming-of-age to become leaders and entrepreneurs. Entrepreneurial ethics can be addressed by establishing a mission statement, business plan, operational procedures and guidelines, and employment contracts and policies (Chittipeddi & Wallett, 1991). Andrews (2014) found that while business ethics are important to millennial entrepreneurs, their decision-making process to start a business did not include business ethics as a factor. Establishing codes of ethics and developing guidelines and strategies to manage ethical dilemmas implemented by entrepreneurs should protect against questionable situations (Bucar, 2001).

Findings and Goals

With the increase of Baby Boomer generation retirements, Millennials already represent the largest generational cohort in the American workforce (Fry, 2015; U.S. Census Bureau, 2015). Organization leaders remain challenged with employment retention and motivation efforts as Millennials tend to have limited long-term commitment to organizations of employment (U.S. Census Bureau, 2014). In a quantitative quasi-experimental study examining cross-generation mentoring, Hechl (2017) found that commitment to retention was most significant for Millennials employees who received cross-generational mentoring. The Hechl study, with a total of 90 male and female Millennial employees from multiple organizations, showed that more than two-thirds of the population received cross-generational mentoring had maintained employment for longer than average periods of times when compared to other Millennial groups. The Hechl findings indicated the significance of devoting workplace assets to development of significant workplace relationships, such as mentoring to encourage increased organization commitment and Millennial motivation. Managers who used both transactional and transformational leadership styles experienced increased retention of Millennial employees (Palechek, 2017).

The use of transformational leadership addresses the strategic issues that managers face when spanning a workforce from Baby Boomers to Millennial (Rowold, 2014). Transformational leadership can transform individual desires to organizational culture of mutual concern by motivating organization members to shift personal perspective for organization commitment (Wren, 1995). Only then can leadership encourage organization members to determine and establish mutually held values and beliefs. Effective leaders choose to become effective leaders (Bass, 1990). Although some leadership skills and personal characteristics develop by chance, to reach higher levels of effectiveness, potential leaders must eventually choose to build skills, clarify values, and develop personally. Without that choosing, any form of leadership development activity will be of limited effectiveness. Motivation of Millennial employees is dependent on the actions of organization leadership.

Focusing on Millennial employee motivational factors, Franklin-Thomas (2016) determined that leadership support of autonomous, flexible work arrangements that were included task specific assignments resulted in stronger motivation and better quality of work life, resulting is stronger commitment to the organization and employee retention. Motivational theories of Maslow's (1954) hierarchy of needs and Herzberg's two-dimensional motivation-hygiene theory aligned well with the findings of Franklin-Thomas, especially regarding leadership practices of motivation, achievement, recognition, responsibility, and advancement. Franklin-Thomas suggested that organization leadership should (a) encourage and support employee development and promotion within the organization, (b) support pursuit of employee interests to enhance employee growth and development, and (c) implement holistic multi-faceted evaluation and feedback programs. Leadership implementation of Millennial-focused organization strategies supports motivation and retention of Millennial employees.

Recommendations

To foster Millennial commitment to an organization, leadership should implement structured employee enrichment and development plans to support career advancement in a challenging autonomous work environment (Alexander & Sysko, 2013). Organization environments and supervisory roles that allow and support flexible work arrangements, flexible hours, and alternative work locations provided better support for achievement in employee development and enhancement (Kultalahti & Viitala, 2014). Leadership is about creating and communicating in understandable language a values-based fabric large enough to encompass the various perceptions and interests of followers, but focused enough to direct all their energies in pursuit of a common cause (Bass, 1990; Wren, 1995). When the leader's vision reflects the needs and aspirations of Millennials and communicated in a manner that brings about understanding—employees become motivated to exceed and succeed.

To foster entrepreneurial success Millennials would do well to use their predilection to moving outside the norms of Boomer tradition. Saravathy's (2001) foundational application of effectuation theory to successful entrepreneurship starts with today's increasingly complex and unpredictable world in concert with the Millennial worldview: the future cannot be assured so it must be made. The use of refractive thinking applies in the situation. Sarasvathy's four basic principles of effectuation continues with: start with the means you have, including who you are, what you know, and who you know. The *bird in hand* principle was by Levi-Strauss in 1967 for the Arts and Sciences, but has found increasingly popular use in the business world, for example, the *Just Do It* of Nike. Setting an affordable loss contrasts with the more conservative estimating the upside of a venture. Successful entrepreneurs, according to Sarasvathy, pursue unknown markets that cannot be analyzed. Being more concerned with the downside of actions to manage risk can be more accurately calculated by serial entrepreneurs, and if they can afford the loss, they take the staged risk.

Saravathy's (2001) third principle of effectuation theory also appears to fit the Millennial ability to bounce back, morph an idea, and start again following a different thread; this is the lemonade principle of leveraging contingencies. Serial entrepreneurs are flexible above all else, ready to move to exploit the unexpected which may not be in existing traditional knowledge. Innovate or die might not matter to a Millennial; the matter may be to get out there and do something different. The final principle of effectuation also fits with Millennial technology skills. Having grown up with communication based on technological means, Millennials might use those skills best to form partnerships via the crazy-quilt principle. Networking is fundamental. Alliances versus isolation lends itself to investor confidence, and with another refractive thinker, can provide even more innovative ideas to foster.

THOUGHTS FROM THE ACADEMIC ENTREPRENEUR

The problem to be solved:

- How to motivate Millennial entrepreneurs
- What traits are necessary for Millennials to become an entrepreneur?

The goals:

- Encouraging and motivating Millennials performance and to avoid attrition

The questions to ask:

- What characteristic traits do Millennials possess as entrepreneurs?
- How can Millennials implement refractive thinking?

Today's Business Application:

- Motivating Millennials in the workforce.
- Developing entrepreneur characteristics and Millennials

REFERENCES

Alexander, C. S., & Sysko, J. M. (2013). I'm gen y, I love feeling entitled, and it shows. *Academy of Educational Leadership Journal, 17*(4), 127-131. Retrieved from http://www.alliedacademies.org/public/journals/journaldetails.aspx?jid=5

Allen, J. (2010). *How a different America responded to the Great Depression.* Pew Research Center. Retrieved from http://www.pewresearch.org/2010/12/14/how-a-different-america-responded-to-the-great-depression/

Andrews, C. (2014). *Business ethics: The role of ethics in the millennial entrepreneurs' decision to start a business.* Available from ProQuest Dissertations and Theses database. (UMI No. 3615108)

Angeline, T. (2011). Managing generational diversity at the workplace: Expectations and perceptions of different generations of employees. *African Journal of Business, 5*(2), 249-255. Retrieved from: http://www.academicjournals.org/journal/AJBM

Bass, B. M. (1990). *Handbook of leadership: Theory, research, and managerial applications* (3rd ed.). New York, NY: The Free Press.

Bott, J., Faulk, D., Guntupalli, A., Devaraj, S., & Holmes, M. (2011). An examination of generational differences and media exposure. *The Journal of Applied Management and Entrepreneurship, 16*(4), 78-100. doi:10.5539/ijbm.v7n24p88

Bovino, B. (2015). *Why millennials and the depression era generation are more similar than you think.* Retrieved from http://fortune.com/2015/04/29/why-millennials-and-the-depression-era-generation-are-more-similar-than-you-think/

Bucar, B. (2001). Ethics of business managers vs. entrepreneurs. *Journal of Developmental Entrepreneurship, 6*, 407-418. doi:10.1007/s10551-005-4674-3

Bursch, D., & Kelly, K. (2014). *Managing the multigenerational workplace.* Retrieved from http://www.kenan-flagler.unc.edu/

Buzz Marketing Group and Young Entrepreneur Council. (2011, January). *Youth entrepreneurship survey.* Retrieved from http://www.slideshare.net/twfashion/yecbuzz-marketing-group-youth-entrepreneurship-study

Charney, D. (2015). *Move over Millennial . . . Now meet generation Z: Material handling and logistics.* Retrieved from http://www.mhlnews.com/

Chittipeddi, K., & Wallett, T.A. (1991). Entrepreneurship and competitive strategy for the1990s. *Journal of Small Business Management, 29*(1), 94-98. doi:10.1007/s11365-009-0108-5

Dennis, H. (2008). *Generations behave differently in the workplace.* Torrance, CA: Daily Breeze.

D'Intino, R., Goldsby, M. G., Houghton, J. D., & Neck, C. P. (2017). Self-leadership: A process for entrepreneurial success, *Journal of Leadership and Organizational Studies,* (13), 4. doi:10.6007/IJARAFMS/v3-i3/178

Dwyer, R. J. (2009). Prepare for the impact of the multi-generational workforce! *Transforming Government: People, Process, and Policy, 3*(2), 101-110. doi:10.1108/17506160910960513

Emeagwali, S. N. (2011). Millennials: Leading the charge for change. *Techniques: Connecting Education and Careers, 86*(5), 22-26. Retrieved from https://eric.ed.gov/?id=EJ925286

Ferri-Reed, J. (2012). Are millennial employees changing how managers manage? *The Journal for Quality & Participation, 37*(2), 15-35. doi:10.1007/s10672-007-9060-0

Franklin-Thomas, S. (2016). *Intrinsic motivational factors of the millennial generation consultants in the professional services workplace.* Available from ProQuest Dissertations & Theses Global. (UMI No. 1775002292)

Friedman, T. (1995). *Making sense of software: Computer games and interactive textuality, in Cybersociety.* Thousand Oaks, CA: Sage.

Fry, R. (2015). *Millennials surpass gen Xers as the largest generation in the U. S. labor force.* Retrieved from http://www.pewresearch.org/

Gardiner, S., Grace, D., & King, C. (2014). The generation effect: The future of domestic tourism in Australia. *Journal of Travel Research, 53*, 705-720. doi:10.1177/0047287514530810

Giannantonio, C. M., & Hurley-Hanson, A. E. (2016). Entrepreneurial characteristics and careers: American high-tech entrepreneurs. *Journal of Business and Management, 2*(2) 59-75, 143-145. Retrieved from https://www.chapman.edu/pdf

Hall, A. S. (2016). Exploring the workplace communication preferences of millennials. *Journal of Organizational Culture, Communications and Conflict, 20*(1), 35-44. doi:10.1007/s10869-010-9172-7

Hamilton, W. (2014). Study: Millennial generation most fiscally cautious since Depression. *Los Angeles Times.* Retrieved from http://articles.latimes.com/

Hammill, G. (2005). Mixing and managing four generations of employees. *FDU Magazine.* Retrieved from http://fdu.edu/newspubs/

Hechl, C. (2017). *Mentoring and affective commitment to organizations: A quantitative comparison study of mentoring functions among millennial employees* (Doctoral dissertation). Available from ProQuest Dissertations & Theses Global. (UMI No. 1882177977)

Heerwagen, J., Kelly, K., & Kampschroer, K. (2016). The changing nature of organizations, work, and workplace. *Whole Building Design Guide.* Retrieved from https://www.wbdg.org/

Hill, R. P. (2002). Managing across generations in the 21st century: Important lessons from the ivory trenches. *Journal of Management Inquiry, 11*(1), 60-66. doi:10.1177/1056492602111020

House, R. J., Hanges, P. J., Ruiz-Quintanilla, A. S., Dorfman, P. W., Javidan,

M., & Dickson, M. W. (1999). Cultural influences in leadership in organizations: Project GLOBE. In W. H. Mobley, M. J. Gessner, and V. Arnold (Eds.), *Advances in global leadership* (pp. 171-233). Stamford, CT: JAI Press.

Hsieh, J. Y. (2016). Spurious or true?: An exploration of antecedents and simultaneity of job performance and job satisfaction across the sectors. *Public Personnel Management, 45*(1), 90-118. Retrieved from http://journals.sagepub.com/home/ppm

Inglehart, R. (1977). *The silent revolution: Changing values and political styles among western publics.* Princeton, NJ: Princeton University Press.

Jacoby, M. (2015). *Tips for managing generations the employees in the workplace.* Retrieved from http://www.huffingtonpost.com/

Kaifi, B. A., Nafei, W. A., Khanfar, N. M., & Kaifi, M. M. (2012). A multi-generational workforce: Managing and understanding millennials. *International Journal of Business and Management, 7*, 88-93. doi:10.5539/ijbm.v7n24p88

Khor, P., & Mapunda, G. (2014, January). A phenomenological study of the lived experiences of the Generation X and Y Entrepreneurs. In *International Conference on Business Strategy and Organizational Behaviour (BizStrategy). Proceedings* (p. 6). Global Science and Technology Forum. Retrieved from http://eprints.uthm.edu.my/3431/1/MGT071.pdf

Kilber, J., Barclay, A., & Ohmer, D. (2014). Seven tips for managing Generation Y. *Journal of Management Policy and Practice, 15*(4), 80-91. doi:10.1108/JMP-08-2014-0230

Kolbe, L. J. (2014). Introductory commentary: A précis on the well-being of young Americans. *Health Promotion Practice, 15*, 5-9. doi:10.1177/1524839913503804

Kultalahti, S., & Viitala, R. L. (2014). Sufficient challenges and a weekend ahead-Generation Y describing motivation at work. *Journal of Organizational Change Management, 27*, 569-582. doi:10.1108/JOCM-05-2014-0101

Leavitt, R. (2014). Generational differences in work motivation of healthcare workers. *Theses, Dissertations, & Student Scholarship: Agricultural Leadership, Education, & Communication Department.* Retrieved from http://digitalcommons.unl.edu/aglecdiss/97/

Leonard, N. H., Beauvais, L. L., & Scholl, R. W. (1999). Work motivation: The incorporation of self-concept-based processes. *Human Relations, 52*, 969-998. doi:10.1023/A:1016927507008

Martin, C. (2017). From high maintenance to high productivity: What managers need to know about Generation Y. *Industrial and Commercial Training, 37*(1), 39-44. doi:10.1108/00197850510699965

Ng, E. S., Schweitzer, L., & Lyons, S. T. (2010). New generation, great expectations: A field study of the Millennial generation, *Journal of Business Psychology, 25*(2), 281-292. doi:10.1007/s10869-010-9159

Ozkan, M., & Solmaz, B. (2015). The changing face of the employees–Generation Z and their perceptions of work (A study applied to university students). *Procedia Economics and Finance, 26,* 476-483. doi:10.1016/S2212-5671(15)00876-X

Palechek, R. P. (2017). *Explaining the moderating effects of job satisfaction on the relationship between employee perceptions of leadership styles and intention to stay for millennial military veterans.* Available from ProQuest Dissertations & Theses Global. (UMI No. 1883884987)

Perkins, S. (2014). When does prior experience pay? Institutional experience and the multinational corporation. *Administrative Science Quarterly, 59,* 145-181. doi:10.1177/0001839214523603

Rezai, M. H., & Rahsepar, T. (2009). Investigating the characteristics of entrepreneurship of IAU students, Darab Branch. *New Approach Quarterly in Educational Management, Second Year. 4,* 45-62. doi:10.1177/0149206309335187

Rowold, J. (2014). Instrumental leadership: Extending the transformational-transactional leadership paradigm. *German Journal of Research in Human Resources, 28,* 367-390. doi:10.1688/ZfP-2014-03-Rowold

Sarasvathy, S. (2001). Causation and effectuation: Toward a theoretical shift from economic inevitability to entrepreneurial contingency. *The Academy of Management Review, 26*(2), 263. Retrieved from http://www.jstor.org/stable/259121

U.S. Census Bureau. (2014). *Employee tenure in 2014.* Retrieved from http://www.bls.gov/news.release/pdf/tenure.pdf

U.S. Census Bureau. (2015). *Millennials outnumber Baby Boomers and are far more diverse.* Retrieved from http://www.census.gov/newsroom/press-releases/2015/cb15113.html

U.S. Department of Labor. (2016). *Employee tenure in 2016.* Retrieved from http://www.bls.gov/news.release/tenure.nr0.htm

Wellner, A. S. (2000). Generational divide: Are traditional methods of classifying a generation still meaningful in a diverse and changing nation? *American Demographics, 22*(10), 52-58. doi:10.3912/OJIN.Vol11No02Man02

Williams, A. (2015). Made Alpha: The next generation. *The New York Times.* Retrieved from https://www.nytimes.com/

Wren, J. T. (1995). *The leader's companion: Insights on leadership through the ages.* New York, NY: The Free Press.

Zarbakhsh, M., Porhassani, S. A., Rahmani, M., Rad, M. M., & Poor, E. K. (2015). The relationship between time management, self-efficacy and entrepreneurship among students. *European Online Journal of Natural and Social Sciences, 4*(1), 211-218. Retrieved from http://european-science.com/eojnss

Zemke, R., Raines, C., & Filipczak, B. (2000). *Generations at work: Managing the clash of Veterans, Boomers, Xers, and Nexters in your workplace.* New York, NY: American Management Association.

About the Authors . . .

Southern California author Dr. Judy Fisher-Blando holds several accredited degrees: a Bachelor of Science (BS) in Business Management; a Master's of Art (MA) in Organizational Management; and a Doctorate of Management (DM) in Organizational Leadership from the University of Phoenix School of Advanced Studies. She has also obtained her Six Sigma Black Belt certificate.

Dr. Judy is an adjunct professor for Walden University, Capella University, and University of Phoenix, teaching classes in organizational behavior, ethical responsibility, and research methods. She is an expert on workplace bullying, writing her research dissertation about *Workplace Bullying: Aggressive Behavior and Its Effect on Job Satisfaction and Productivity*. In addition, she is a Life Coach, coaching leaders on how to develop High Performance Organizations, coaching the targets of workplace bullies, and giving presentations on Finding and Measuring your Joy.

To reach Dr. Judy Fisher-Blando for information on any of these topics, and for executive coaching or coaching for workplace bullying, please e-mail judyblando@gmail.com

Dr. Gayle Grant, a native New Yorker and current Arizona resident holds several accredited degrees, a Bachelor of Arts (BA) from Rutgers University, A Master of Arts (MA) from Kean University, a Doctorate of Management (DM) in Organizational Leadership from University of Phoenix, School of Advanced Studies.

Dr. Gayle (known to her students as 'Doc') is a university professor in Information Technologies, Business, Leadership, Business Management, Marketing, Quality Processes, Project Management, and Doctoral Research with University of Phoenix, Grand Canyon University, Walden University, and Capella University. Dr. Gayle additionally holds various roles with these universities including; mentor, dissertation chair, research methodologist, content committee expert, doctoral residency and intensive residency instructor, University Research Reviewer, lead faculty member, master chair/faculty coach, curriculum consultant and developer. Further, Dr. Gayle owns dual consulting practices specializing in higher education as well as business management / operations / strategic and tactical planning. 'Doc' is an avid investor, web marketer, and enjoys all things entrepreneurial.

Dr. Gayle has previously published in the areas of IT Entrepreneurship, Corporate Social Responsibility, and Web Enabled Doctoral Program Interfaces for Students, Faculty, and Staff. 'Doc' rounds out any remaining time golfing, working out, partaking in various electronic and art related projects as well as sharing her home with her five rescue dogs.

To reach Dr. Gayle Grant for information on any of these topics, please email: gayle.grant@cox.net

Northern California author, Dr. D.Marie Hanson holds several accredited degrees: a Bachelor of Arts (BA) in English Writing and Literature; a Masters of Clinical Psychology; a Master's of Education & Training (MAE/T); and a Doctorate of Psychology (PhD) in Consciousness Studies. Dr. D. is an adjunct professor for Walden University and University of Southern California, mentoring doctoral students as their Chair in the development, research, and writing of their dissertations. She is an expert on consciousness and its impact on life transition and the achievement of major goals. In addition, she is a Life Coach, coaching fellow Boomers in their transition to lives of vibrancy and meaning as elders.

To reach Dr. Hanson for information on any of these topics, and for life transition coaching, e-mail drdmarie5@gmail.com

Dr. Denise L. Land holds the following accredited degrees, including a Bachelor of Science (BS) in Gerontology and Masters of Social Work from California State University, Sacramento; and a Doctorate of Management (DM) in Organizational Leadership from the University of Phoenix School of Advanced Studies. Dr. D., as she is known to her students, is a university professor on faculty at the University of Phoenix, where she also serves as a faculty trainer and mentor. Faculty teaching activities include strategic planning, leadership, and research methods. In addition to her faculty work, she also has university faculty experience in the areas of human services, psychology, communications, research, management, leadership, doctoral research, and critical thinking. Additional published works include her dissertation: Identifying Strategic Leadership Practice Motivators of Nonprofit Employee Retention; and "Socio-Technical Systems Advancement: Making Distance Learning Changes That Count" Journal of U.S. Distance Learning Association.

To reach Dr. Denise Land for information on any of these topics, please e-mail: drdlland@gmail.com

 Dr. Huong Ly holds the following accredited degrees: Bachelor of Science in Medical Technology from the State University of New York at Plattsburgh; a Master of Business Administration in Health Care Administration from Ellis University; and a Doctorate of Business Administration in Leadership from Walden University. In addition, she is also a certified Six Sigma Green Belt and a qualified auditor for International Organization for Standard.

Dr. Holly, as she prefers to be called, is currently a laboratory manager at Kaiser Permanente. Prior to joining Kaiser Permanente, she was an operational manager at Focus Diagnostics Inc., a subsidiary of Quest Diagnostics Inc. In this role, she was able to increase the quality of laboratory service while reducing operational costs. The ultimate challenge that exhibits her leadership skill was her role as manager of quality assurance at Focus Diagnostics Inc. Here she further honed her skills in project management and effective interpersonal communication. This position was particularly challenging due to employees unrest related to a pending physical relocation of the laboratory, yet she helped employees focused on the company's commitment to quality. Through these roles, she acquired the reasoning, leadership, and communication skills for her role as coordinator for the newly-created Focus Diagnostics Inc. medical technologist training school. In this position, she gained first-hand experience developing an effective teaching program and communicating with students.

To reach Dr. Holly for information pertaining to any of these topics, please email: drhollyly@gmail.com

CHAPTER 2

The Relationship Between Hardiness and Entrepreneurship

Dr. Jennifer Smith

Many microbusinesses (sole proprietors, entrepreneurs, and small businesses) consisting of 20 or fewer employees (U.S. Small Business Association [U.S, SBA], 2013) enter the market annually. The term business owners included entrepreneurs because entrepreneurs are business owners who may own several business ventures or may operate as a sole proprietor. The U.S. SBA (2013) reported 27.9 million small businesses in the United States, of which three-quarters were sole-proprietors. The U.S. SBA (2013) reported 2.1 million small businesses in Texas, of which 83.1% represented sole proprietorships, which closely modeled the U.S. numbers. Small business startups averaged 22,000 per quarter and small business closings averaged 20,800 per quarter, supporting the fact that business survival remains a challenge for entrepreneurs and small business owners (Smith, 2015). Similar to how leaders are cultivated for success (Roudy, 2012), psychological hardiness must be cultivated for entrepreneurial success (Smith, 2015). The relationship between psychological hardiness and entrepreneurial are examined further in this chapter.

The business owners surveyed included sole proprietors (included entrepreneurs in this group), and businesses with 20 or fewer employees (Smith, 2015). The number of business closures in the market is equal to or surpasses the number of business startups (Knaup, 2005), indicating survival within the market is a challenge for the business owner. External factors impact business success, but the focus for this research was how the internal factor, psychological hardiness, impacted business success. Empirical research identified psychological hardiness as an effective predictor of success in nursing, the military, academia, and a variety of other fields (Bartone, 2008; Chamorro-Premuzic & Furnham, 2003; Jasra, Khan, Hungary, Rahman, & Azam, 2011). Other research results indicated psychological hardiness as a contributing factor to business success (Fisher, Maritz, & Lobo, 2016; Ghule & Shejwal, 2016; Smith, 2015). Maddi and Kobasa (1998) identified psychological hardiness as personal characteristics individuals utilize in stressful situations to (a) enhance performance, (b) strengthen leadership, (c) improve conduct, (d) improve health, and (e) for psychological growth. Additional traits noted as contributors to business performance include adaptability, optimism, and internal locus of control (Owens, 2003). Little or no empirical research exists regarding internal factors, specifically psychological hardiness, and the relationship to business owner success among entrepreneurs, sole proprietors, and small business owners. Empirical research indicates that financial issues, money mismanagement, and other external factors directly impact business success (Alsaaty, 2012). The focus of the study was to explore internal factors, specifically hardiness traits, and the relationship to business success instead of studying external factors known to impact business success. Focusing on the internal factors, which is outside of the usual parameters of focus for success, provides a different perspective for business owners regarding business success. Cultivation of leaders is important in an organization for growth (Roudy, 2010). The Smith study (2015) proposed cultivation of hardiness traits as equally important to entrepreneurial and small business success. The focus of this research was to determine if a correlation existed between psychological hardness and small business owner success and to evaluate the characteristics business owners attributed to success (Smith, 2015). Business owners may be able to improve business survival rates if they understood the relationship between psychological hardiness and business success.

Exploring Psychological Hardiness

Microbusinesses experience survival challenges within the first 5 years of opening. Empirical research also indicated that the survival rate for microbusinesses decreased with time over the 5 year span (Alsaaty, 2012; Knapp, 2005). Businesses had a survival rate of 66% from inception to 2 years (entering at a rate of 22,000 and closing at a rate of 20,800), which decreased to a 44% survival rate within 4 years of inception (Knaup, 2005). Smith (2015) indicated the general focus of the study was to evaluate how the owner's psychological hardiness contributed to business success. Business owners must have a commitment to work, believe they have control over or influence the success of the business, and embrace challenges (Maddi, 2007).

Prior empirical research indicated a connection between psychological hardiness to business owner success and work performance (Fahed-Sreih & Morin-Delerm, 2012; Jasra, Khan, Hungary, Rahman, & Azam, 2011; Kobasa, 1979; Maddi, 2007; Owens, 2003). The fore-mentioned studies referenced the hardiness traits within the workplace; however, literary research provided little or no empirical research regarding psychological hardiness and small business owner success (Smith, 2015). The purpose of the study was to determine if a correlation existed between psychological hardiness and microbusiness owner success and identify any significant differences in hardiness by (a) experience, (b) present age, (c) gender, and (d) ethnicity (Smith, 2015). The concept explored was that microbusiness success depends on the psychological hardiness of the owner. Educational institutions may use the results in classes, training programs, workshops designed to provide microbusiness owners with the tools to increase hardiness and the likelihood of business success (Smith, 2015). The results also provide the foundation for continued research to make results generalizable to the microbusiness population.

The focus of the Smith (2015) study was on the following questions and hypothesis.

R1. What is the correlation between psychological hardiness and business owner success?

The definition for success included operating for a minimum of two years with revenue exceeding expenses. The possibility exists for microbusiness owners to reduce business closures and achieve a higher level of success by strengthening hardiness traits. Kobasa (1979) noted commitment, control, and challenge (psychological hardiness traits) to be effective predictors of success within other fields. If psychological hardiness traits are effective predictors of success in other fields, hardiness traits may be effective predictors of business owner success.

The expectation was a positive correlation between psychological hardiness and small business owner success would exist based on Kobasa's (1979) theory that psychological hardiness is an effective predictor of success.

R2. How does psychological hardiness differ with reference to experience (whether the person has been successful in business after previous failure)?

Kobasa (1979) identified control as one of the three Cs of psychological hardiness, where the individual understands that he or she has some influence or control over situations. The hardiness trait, control, for the business owner would indicate that experiencing failure is a growth opportunity and not a deterrent from pursuing other business opportunities. Each growth opportunity (failure) would allow the business owner to analyze and determine the most effective strategy for the next business venture.

Kobasa's (1979) theory noted that individuals learn from prior situations and turn adverse situations into growth opportunities. The expectation was individuals would have a higher score for the control trait if they experienced prior business failures. Based on this assumption the business owner would utilize opportunities to learn from prior failures and strategize differently when pursuing other business ventures.

R3. How does psychological hardiness differ with reference to present age of the owner?

The assumption was older participants increased their knowledge base (more life and work experiences to draw from), resulting in a higher psychological hardiness score than younger participants with less work and life experiences from which to draw. Empirical research revealed that students mature (21 years and older) in age had higher scores than the younger individuals (Sheard, 2009). The Smith study (2015) indicated 40 as the mature age within the workplace in accordance to the reference in Lacy's (2005) study which categorized individuals 40 years and up in the older or mature group. The expectation was owners mature in age would have a higher level of hardiness based on a knowledge based gained from prior experiences and the ability to turn each experience into a growth opportunity. Kobasa (1979) noted one of the psychological traits included the ability to learn from prior experiences.

R4. How does psychological hardiness differ with reference to gender of the owner?

The expectation was that a significant difference would exist in business owners by gender. Sheard (2009) revealed women scored higher than their male counterparts academically and Craft (1999) determined women believed that outcomes are a direct result of actions, resulting in an increased level of hardiness through the control trait. Loscocco and Bird (2012) revealed that women were not as profitable in small business as men because of distractions such as family life and nurturing sick family members. The female and male participants in this study had comparable levels of success to avoid unequal comparisons.

R5. How does psychological hardiness differ with reference to ethnicity of the owner?

Pattie, Parks, and Wales (2012) found that Caucasian owned businesses experienced less failures and succeeded at a faster rate than did the non-Caucasian owned businesses. Pattie et al. attributed the differences in the level of success to the difference in cultural values regarding security. The assumption was, based on the findings of Pattie et al. (2012), the results indicating a difference in hardiness scores by ethnicity. The expectation was, minorities faced more challenges resulting in failures than Caucasian counterparts which would increase the level of hardiness in minorities.

R6. What characteristics, strategies, and attitudes do small business owners attribute to their success?

The assumption was that there would be a pattern in the qualities, characteristics, and strategies identified by business owners as contributing to their success. The expectation was that the traits identified by business owners would align with the psychological hardiness traits identified by Kobasa (1979).

Theoretical Framework

The basis for exploring the correlation between psychological hardiness and small business owner success derived from Kobasa's (1979) introduction of resiliency, or hardiness, as a predictor of success. Hardiness or resiliency, a psychological construct, allows individuals the ability to be resilient amidst adversity and turn adverse situations into an opportunity for growth. Maddi (2007) and Kobasa noted that individuals had the ability to utilize the hardiness characteristics during stressful situations to (a) enhance performance, (b) for leadership, (c) change behaviors, (d) cope with health challenges, and (e) for psychological growth. The theory behind the research was psychological hardiness traits were essential to small business owner success. The term hardiness traits referred to the traits identified by Kobasa, Maddi, and Kahn (1982) as commitment, challenge, and control.

Even though little or no empirical research existed regarding hardiness traits and small business owner success, previous empirical research indicated that hardiness traits effectively predicted individual success in the military forces (Bartone, Roland, Picano, & Williams, Maddi, 2007), nursing (Hurst & Koplin-Baucum, 2005), academia (Chamorro-Premuzic & Furnham, 2003), and several other areas as well. Research conducted in the military indicated individuals with high hardiness levels correlated with an increase in individual performance (Bartone, Roland, Picano, & Williams, 2008; Skomorovsky & Sudom, 2011). Maddi (2007) concluded that hardiness training would be beneficial for individuals in high-level stress positions and would benefit a variety of fields, if implemented. The Smith study (2015) results indicate a relationship between psychological traits and business owner success exists; however, the results are not generalizable because of the small sample size. Based on the results of the study (Smith, 2015), resiliency is an important factor in business success.

The first introduction to the concept of psychological hardiness included research at the Illinois Bell Telephone Company (IBTC) by Maddi (2002) and a team of researchers. The focus of the study conducted at IBTC explored the concept that hardiness traits may contribute to the avoidance of health issues related to stress (Maddi, 2007). Kobasa et al. (1982) identified commitment, control, and challenge as psychological hardiness traits, also defined as the three Cs of psychological hardiness. The identified traits remain relevant to microbusiness owners as well. Microbusiness owners must commit to business success and growth; and utilize adverse situations for personal development and growth.

Hardiness was a contributing factor to commitment within the medical field (Hurst & Koplin-Baucum, 2005). A difference in hardiness levels was evident based on the level of position within the medical field. Nursing assistants had lower psychological hardiness levels than the registered nurses. Mentors who exhibited strong psychological hardiness traits had the ability to pass these traits on to the mentees (Hurst & Koplin-Baucum, 2005). Psychological hardiness levels were higher in the academia setting for the females and those more mature in age, than their male counterparts (Sheard, 2009). Similar research conducted in the military by Skomorovsky and Sudom (2011) indicated individuals (both female and male) with higher hardiness levels also had higher levels of satisfaction with training, and experienced less stress.

Many business owners experience a myriad of challenges, which may contribute to business closures including, but not limited to: cultural differences (Alsaaty, 2012), barriers to the market, finances (Mouly & Sankaran, 2004), and, other adverse situations (Sam, 2007). Microbusiness owners (including entrepreneurs) may experience difficulties when conducting business with individuals committed to their cultural values. Understanding other cultural beliefs and accommodating individuals committed to such values requires the business owner to have the ability to adapt to change. Hardiness traits such as commitment and challenge may allow the business owner to focus on adapting and changing, instead of alienation, to be successful within that culture. When faced with the challenge of adverse situations, the business owner should have the commitment to face the challenge and utilize their level of control to reverse the situation or capitalize on the situation for growth (Smith, 2015).

Methodology

The mixed method approach allows for the study of a phenomenon in more detail and combines qualitative and quantitative methods to collect data (Venkateesh, Brown, & Bala, 2013). The results of the quantitative analysis determined if small business owner success depended on the psychological hardiness of the small business owner and to evaluate if there was a significant difference between psychological hardiness with reference to: (a) experience, (b) present age, (c) ethnicity, or, (d) gender of the owner. The results of the qualitative analysis determined if patterns existed in the self-identified characteristics, strategies, and attitudes by small business owners as contributors to business success. The scores from the 15-item Dispositional Resilience Scale (DRS-15), a hardiness assessment, provided the quantitative information and responses from the survey provided the qualitative.

Participants provided demographic information, characteristics, attitudes, and strategies self-identified by business owners as contributing to their success. Participants then completed the DRS-15, a psychological hardiness assessment, which indicated hardiness levels. The targeted population consisted of microbusiness owners from the Dallas / Fort Worth (DFW) Metroplex, who operated at least one business in the Metroplex and had been in business for over 2 years, with at least the current or both fiscal years yielding a profit, with 20 or fewer employees (includes sole proprietors and entrepreneurs). The DFW patterns closely model the statistics from other states in the United States. The criterion for participation was the same for both the qualitative and quantitative portions of the study. The total sample size from DFW consisted of 128 entrepreneurs and small business owners.

Findings

The quantitative findings indicated that no statistically significant differences in psychological hardiness scores by age, p [greater than] .05 (Smith, 2015). Statistically significant differences were determined to be present if p [less than] .05 (Smith, 2015). The findings indicated statistically significant differences in psychological hardiness scores by experience, gender, and ethnicity, and in the psychological hardiness sub-scale scores by ethnicity, p [less than] .05. The findings did not indicate a correlation between psychological hardiness and small business owner success; however, some unexpected factors such as faith in God (God in control instead of the individual in control), could have skewed the Hardiness scores. The qualitative analyses indicated that business owners identified similar characteristics, business strategies, and traits. These findings met the expectation proposed by Smith (2015) that a relationship existed between psychological hardiness and business owner success. These findings indicate business owners rely on faith that God is in control instead of relying on self.

An unusual circumstance encountered during the data collection process occurred when business owners completing the DRS-15 assessment were uncertain how to respond to questions in the control sub-scale due to the belief that "God was in control of everything" (Smith, 2015, p. 78). Sixty-five percent (83) of the 128 participants noted this conflict when responding to the control questions on the DRS-15. Therefore, some participants hesitated to answer questions that asked if they felt they were in control of their life (Smith, 2015). Therefore, the results of the DRS-15 do not directly represent the true hardiness level of the business owners. Business owners, who had faith, relied on God as the one in control and directly involved with the results of the individual's actions.

Business owners identified the following as the top three

characteristics, strategies, and attitudes as contributors to business success: commitment (34%), control (27%), and challenge (15%). Other characteristics, strategies, and attitudes self-identified by business owners as contributors to business success (in order of importance): personality, skills, education, faith, workers, financial management, reward, failures, and support systems. The results of this research are intended to provide a foundation for continued research regarding psychological hardiness and small business owner success utilizing a difference sampling method to allow results to be more generalizable within the small business community.

Conclusion

The Smith (2015) study indicated a correlation between hardiness and entrepreneurial/small business owner success. Further analysis indicated that faith in God may have impacted hardiness scores resulting in analysis did not indicate a correlation between hardiness scores and success, but further analyses indicated that faith in God may have impacted hardiness scores. The results revealed owners identified similar traits as major contributors to business success. The top traits identified indicated commitment (full involvement of the individual), control (not feeling helpless in adverse situations; the ability to act and change outcomes), and challenge (understanding that change is inevitable and dealing with it in a positive way) as major contributors to success. These top traits identified by small business owners as contributing to business success are the same traits identified by Kobasa (1979) as psychological hardiness traits. Therefore, the results indicate small business owners associate hardiness traits with success. Owners also identified personality, skills, education, experience, faith, workers, financial management, reward, failures, and support systems as contributors to business success (Smith, 2015).

The Smith (2015) study revealed a correlation between hardiness and success. Further analysis indicated differences existed in hardiness scores by gender, ethnicity, and in the subscales commitment, control, and challenge, based on number of years in business, and by gender and ethnicity (Smith, 2015). These findings provide insight into the traits entrepreneurs and small business owners attribute to business success, which align with the psychological hardiness traits as identified by Kobasa (1979) as predictive indicators of success. These findings provide a foundation for continued research, perhaps including faith as a contributing factor. The focus of the Smith (2015) study is unique because at the time, few or no studies focused on internal factors as contributors to business success among entrepreneurs, sole proprietors, and small business owners. Refractive thinking is thinking beyond the box, and as shown in this study, focusing on the internal factors along with external factors provides a complete understanding of what contributes to business success. Organizational growth occurs by cultivating leaders Roudy (2010). The Smith (2015) study indicated entrepreneurial and small business owner success occurs by cultivating hardiness traits.

THOUGHTS FROM THE ACADEMIC ENTREPRENEUR

The problem to be solved:

- Thriving in the business sector remains a challenge for entrepreneurs and small business owners.

The goals:

- For small business owners and entrepreneurs to understand the psychological factors that contribute to business owner success and utilize resources to improve hardiness.

The questions to ask:

- How can business owners be successful in the business sector?
- Can focusing on strengthening psychological hardiness traits help business owners be more successful?

Today's Business Application:

- The following psychological hardiness traits are major contributors to entrepreneurial and business success: commitment, control, and challenge.
- Entrepreneurs and small business owners should constantly reassess the level of commitment, their ability to adapt to situations, and face challenges to identify areas for improvement on a continual basis.
- Business owners should seek to improve in these areas through training and workshops.

REFERENCES

Alsaaty, F. M. (2012). The cycle of births and deaths of U.S. employer micro firms. *Journal of Management & Marketing Research, 11*, 1-12. Retrieved from http://www.aabri.com/

Bartone, P. (2007a). Test-retest reliability of the Dispositional Resilience Scale-15: A brief hardiness scale. *Psychological Reports, 101*, 943-944. doi:10.2466/pr0.101.7.943-944

Bartone, P. T. (2007b). *Dispositional Resilience Scale Assessment (DRS15v3)*. Retrieved from http://www.kbmetrics.com

Bartone, P. T., Roland, R. R., Picano, J. J., & Williams, T. J. (2008). Psychological hardiness predicts success in U.S. Army Special Forces candidates. *International Journal of Selection and Assessment, 16*(1), 78-81. doi:10.1111/j.1468-2389.2008.00412.x

Chamorro-Premuzic, T., & Furnham, A. (2003). Personality predicts academic performance: Evidence from two longitudinal university samples. *Journal of Research in Personality, 46*, 319-338. doi:10.1016/S0092-6566(02)00578-0

Craft, C. (1999). A conceptual model of feminine hardiness. *Holistic Nursing Practice, 13*(3), 25-34. doi:10.1097/00004650-199904000-00006

Deuster, P. A., & Silverman, M. N. (2013). Physical fitness: A pathway to health and resilience. *U.S. Army Medical Journal*, 24-35. Retrieved from http://www.cs.amedd.org.mil

DiCicco-Bloom, B., & Crabtree, B. (2006). The qualitative research interview. *Medical Education, 40*, 314-321. doi:10.1111/j.1365-2929.2006.02418.x

Fahed-Sreih, J., & Morin-Delerm, S. (2012). A perspective on leadership in small businesses: Is the need for achievement a motive in predicting success? *International Journal of Entrepreneurship, 16*, 1-23. Retrieved from http://www.alliedacademies.org

Ghule, V., & Shejwal, B.R. (2016). The role of cognitive hardiness in health and performance of bank managers. *Indian Journal of Health & Wellbeing, 7*, 383-387. Retrieved from http://www.iahrw.com

Hurst, S., & Koplin-Baucum, S. (2005). A pilot qualitative study relating to hardiness in ICU: Hardiness in ICU nurses. *Dimensions of Critical Care Nursing: DCCN, 24*(2), nurses 97-100. doi:10.1097/00003465-200503000-00011

Jasra, J., Khan, M., Hunjra, A., Rehman, R., & Azam, R. (2011). Determinants of business success of small and medium enterprises. *International Journal of Business & Social Science, 2*(20), 274-280. Retrieved from http://www.ijbssnet.com

Johnsen, B. H., Bartone, P., Sandvik, A. M., Gjeldnes, R., Morken, A. M., Hystad, S. W., & Stornaes, A. V. (2013). Psychological hardiness predicts success in a

Norwegian armed forces border patrol selection course. *International Journal of Selection & Assessment, 21,* 368-375, doi:10.1111/ijsa.120

Knaup, A. E. (2005). Survival and longevity in the business employment dynamics data. *Monthly Labor Review, 128*(5), 50-56. Retrieved from http://www.bls.gov/

Kobasa, S. C. (1979). Stressful life events, personality, and health: An inquiry into hardiness. *Journal of Personality and Social Psychology, 37*(1), 1-11. doi:10.1037//0022-3514.37.1.1

Kobasa, S. C., Maddi, S. R., & Kahn, S. (1982). Hardiness and health: A prospective study. *Journal of Personality and Social Psychology, 42*(1), 169-177. doi:10.1037//0022-3514.42.1.168

Lacy, D. A. (2005). You are not quite as old as you think: Making the case for reverse age discrimination under the ADEA. *Berkeley Journal of Employment & Labor Law, 26,* 363-403. doi:10.157791238534

Loscocco, K., & Bird, S. R. (2012). Gendered paths: Why women lag behind men in small business success. *Work & Occupations, 39*(2), 183-219. doi:10.1177/0730888412444282

Maddi, S. R. (2002). The story of hardiness: Twenty years of theorizing, research, and practice. *Consulting Psychology Journal: Practice and Research, 54*(3), 173-185. doi:10.1037/1061-4087.54.3.173

Maddi, S. R. (2007). Relevance of hardiness assessment and training to the military context. *Military Psychology, 19*(1), 61–70. doi:10.1080/08995600701323301

Mouly, V., & Sankaran, J. K. (2004). Survival and failure of small businesses arising through government privatization: Insights from two New Zealand firms. *Journal of Management Studies, 41,* 1435-1467. doi:10.1111/j.1467-6486.2004.00481.x

Owens, K. S. (2003). *An investigation of the personality correlates of small business success* (Doctoral dissertation). Retrieved from ProQuest Dissertations and Theses Database. (UMI No. 3119293)

Pattie, M., Parks, L., & Wales, W. (2012). Who needs security?: Entrepreneurial minorities, security values, and firm performance. *Journal of Management Inquiry, 21,* 319-328, doi:10.1177/1056492611425090n

Roudy, C. A. (2010). Chapter 4: Behavioral integrity: The precursor to ethical leadership. *In Refractive thinker: Volume IV: Ethics, leadership, and globalization* (pp. 65-80). Las Vegas, NV: Lentz Leadership Institute LLC.

Sam, M. A. (2007). Surviving the years of infancy: Longevity among small firms in Nigeria, 1971–1997. *Journal of International Development, 19,* 1023-1042. doi:10.1002/jid.1359

Sheard, M. (2009). Hardiness commitment, gender, and age differentiate university academic performance. *British Journal of Educational Psychology, 79*(1), 189-204. doi:10.1348/000709908x304406

Skomorovsky, A., & Sudom, K. A. (2011). Role of hardiness in the psychological well-being of Canadian forces officer candidates. *Military Medicine, 176*(1), 7-12. doi:10.7205/milmed-d-10-00325

Smith, J. (2015). *Exploring the relationship between psychological hardiness and small business owner success* (Doctoral dissertation). Retrieved from ProQuest Dissertations and Theses Global. (UMI No. 3706239)

U.S. Small Business Administration. (2013). Advocacy: The voice of small business in government. *Small Business Profile.* Retrieved from http://www.sba.gov/sites/default/files/tx12.pdf

Venkatesh, V., Brown, S. A., & Bala, H. (2013). Bridging the qualitative-quantitative divide: Guidelines for conducting mixed methods research in information systems. *MIS Quarterly, 37*(1), 21-54. Retrieved from http://misq.org/

White, D. W., Absher, R., & Huggins, K. A. (2011). The effects of hardiness and cultural distance on socio-cultural adaptation in an expatriate sales manager population. *Journal of Personal Selling & Sales Management, 31,* 325-338. doi:10.2753/pss0885-3134310309

About the Author . . .

Dr. Jennifer Smith resides in the historic town of Red Oak, Texas. Dr. Jennifer, affectionately known as *Doc J* to her students, is adjunct faculty at Cedar Valley College, Dr. Jennifer also teaches at local Co-ops and for several nonprofit organizations. Dr. Jennifer serves on the board for several nonprofit organizations and is passionate about serving the community. She is also the principal business consultant for 3AM Consulting Services.

Dr. Jennifer is also an active member of Society of Industrial Psychologists.

To reach Dr. Jennifer Smith for information on entrepreneurial workshops, business consulting, or guest speaking, please visit her website: http://www.3amconsultingservices.com or e-mail: drjsmith@3amconsultingservices.com

CHAPTER 3

Everything to Everybody: What Does Your Business Do?

Dr. Ivan Salaberrios

The identity of the company is like an individual's character. Reputation in a business-to-business industry supports a company's identity (Wiersema, 2013). A company's reputation promotes an identity based on the company's capabilities. Capabilities describe the services or products the company produces (Teece, 2012). Over time, companies need to adapt, adjust, and tweak their corporate capabilities to meet market demands (Beske, 2012). Overall, customer satisfaction drives companies to improve their services as well. In some cases, such changes in capabilities result in positive rewards for entrepreneurs (Srivastava & Rai, 2014). The results of change reward companies by allowing them to conduct business in another channel of the revenue stream. The specific problem is the effect of businesses changing their capabilities make the companies operate outside of their comfort zone and risking failure. Business leaders realize the consequences of failure because the company focuses on overall customer satisfaction instead of providing the services or products within its mastered core capabilities (Sarin, 2014). An entrepreneur, using a refractive thinking approach, can navigate around the pitfalls that many companies encounter. By thinking outside of the box, a new entrepreneur stands a better chance to avoid one of small business's silent killers such as unexpected growth.

Upon entry to the market place, businesses start out as an unknown brand (Mazodier & Merunka, 2012). The brand is their name, reputation, or description of the way the company does business. The strength of their brand mirrors the quality and results of their services products (Goel & Ramesh, 2016). Within 2 years of launching a new company, the brand of the business builds recognition through its own operations. The brand gets stronger and better recognized. (Upamannyu, Sankpal, & Gupta, 2015). According to a study by Wan, Chen, and Yiu (2015), growing companies need to focus on their identity. As time passes, companies establish a market or corporate identity. The same companies do not measure the status of their corporate identity and lack understanding of the actual value of the identity (Roberts & Arachchige, 2015).

Business professionals confuse brand with corporate identity often (Robertson & Khatibi, 2012). A difference between a brand and a corporate identity exists. Corporate identity is the overall result of multiple factors (Hautz, Mayer, & Stadler, 2013). Factors include reputation, customer satisfaction, customer base acknowledgment, and customer loyalty (Galia, 2015). Each of the combined factors help form a corporate identity. Similar to strengthening a brand, building a corporate identity takes 5 years to establish. Larger companies reach such a milestone through less business maturation.

Entrepreneurs face challenges growing their business and become conflicted between remaining the kind company they expect or becoming something different, larger, and acceptable to existing and new clients (Lin & Piercy, 2012). The challenge of entrepreneurship evolves from the time of business infancy to maturity. In the United States, most businesses fail within 10 years (U.S. Small Business Administration, 2012). A decade is a long time to exist as a company to then only fail. A common cause of a mature company's failure is the company's inability to grow (Bischoff & Wood, 2013). Looking to the future, small business owners have access to more tools and faster market entry (Solomon, 2012). More tools help entrepreneurs make better decisions by solving traditional complex business problems (Bischoff & Wood, 2013). A clear path to market entry makes the future of small business brighter for entrepreneurs looking to grow their business (Lin & Piercey, 2012). Refractive thinking encourages the examination of old data through a new lens. Using a refractive approach helps entrepreneurs to maintain business continuity by implementing change management, an overlooked business practice. Thinking outside of the box allows inexperienced business owners to successfully navigate change by building on the experience of past business owners (Schuttler & Lentz, 2013).

Overview of Study

The study of growing businesses managing changing identity includes established entrepreneurs running a small products and services business. Decisions overwhelm entrepreneurs daily (Robertson & Khatibi, 2012). Business owners do not focus on long-term strategies (Webb, 2014). More seasoned business owners have the primary task of steering companies towards a long-term goal. According to Robertson and Khatibi (2012), as simple as making decisions may sound, rendering decisions determine the overall result of a business. Growing companies encounter mission creep. Research about mission creep includes studies of companies slowly derailed by moving away from their core competency (Fischer, 2012). Growth opportunities emerge from long standing business relationships (Singh, 2015). When business leaders see a chance to grow, they must consider mission creep. The company needs to stray away from their core competency to satisfy the emerging opportunities (Beske, 2012). Pursuing new growth opportunities creates a gap between the core capabilities and the new capabilities.

Mission creep is a military term that indicates a particular mission slowly changes because of unforeseen challenges and adjustments (Heesacker, 2005). The term mission creep emerged into a business phrase used to describe corporate organizations knowingly straying away from their core competency. Businesses mostly change their capabilities to meet growing demand and customized services requests (Engelbrekt, 2015). When growing a small business, by expanding capabilities, a company risks diminishing its identity when the changes are not managed properly.

Some companies intentionally change their identity to improve perception in the market (Chen, Chi, & Friedman, 2013). According to Fischer (2012), such rebranding initiatives are not considered mission creep, which is similar to project management scope creep or software development function creep. Scope creep is the process of adding tasks to a project scope of work after the completion of the planning stage. Function creep deals with scope creep during software development projects (Thakurta, 2013). Small business owners must maintain alignment with their company's performance to their long-term strategic goals (Jahromi, Stakhovych, & Ewing, 2014). By allowing the business's market identity to diminish, the company risks brand trust, as well as diminished credibility with their client base. The success of business-to-business branding is sensitive to maintaining a reputation of quality (Hemel, 2016). In business-to-business relationships, small businesses cannot risk losing credibility or gaining a reputation of brand ambiguity (Chen et al., 2013). In business, as in life, change must be managed properly. Proper planning and customer buy-in can help a company to create change within their own corporate identity by emerging with different service or product offerings (Walsh, Evanschitzky, Schaarschmidt, Walgenbach, & Beatty, 2016). This chapter indicates many risks exist when growing a company. Small businesses can manage the identity gaps when pursuing opportunities in emerging markets. Identifying the risks and managing change help entrepreneurs pursue new opportunities without closing their doors (Beske, 2012).

Trying to be *everything to everybody* can hurt business (Srivastava & Rai, 2014). Business leaders can lose focus on the company's mission by chasing opportunities with very thin rewards. Businesses cannot be everything to everyone, however a company can expand business offerings to meet the most lucrative market demands (Helfat & Martin, 2015). Business leaders must learn to cater to their best customers, as well as their emerging customer base that will pay the bills for tomorrow (Downes & Nunes, 2013).

Background Theory

Most business professionals are aware of the statistics hosted by the U.S. Small Business Administration (SBA) (2015) regarding the viability of small businesses within 5 years. Over half of small businesses fail within the first 5 years (U.S. Small Business Administration [SBA], 2015). A little over two thirds of startup businesses fail within the first year (U.S. Census Bureau, 2015). The U.S. Small Business Administration cited failures such as insufficient capital or experience. Most business professionals have an understanding of business failures and are helpful in navigating through financial and experience challenges (Preechanont & Tao, 2013). Investors perceive growth as a good problem to have because it allows companies additional options previously unexpected (Bischoff & Wood, 2013). According to SBA (2015), unexpected growth is a factor that causes business failure within 5 years. Small and mid-size businesses are not prepared to handle growth. Entrepreneurs do not have the resources to obtain proper access to capital or experience to lead a company through unexpected growth (Salaberrios, 2016). How can business growth kill your business? If growing a business results in additional revenue, how can earning more money be a risk to your business? The goal of this chapter is to address these questions. The chapter includes a review of business growth related issues that may make sense of how business growth can be detrimental to the success of the company (Lin & Piercy, 2012).

Mission Creep

Mission creep is a term used to describe a problem with business operations, as well as major projects (Heesacker, 2005). Mission creep is different than scope creep in a sense that scope creep only deals with project management (Thakurta, 2013). Function creep, also known as feature creep, means changes in the scope of work with software development projects (Goldstein, Bergman, & Maier, 2013). Mission creep is a challenge primarily associated with business growth (Fischer, 2012). Many companies exhaust most of their resources and scatter the company's primary skill sets. When a firm's resources distribute all over the market, the company appears to have little experience. Scattered resources and skill sets lead to weaker commitments and a higher cost of time and money to their core competency business (Fischer, 2012). The spreading resources give leaders the illusion of wider market coverage. Scattering resources with the company's primary skill sets lessen customer's firm future commitment to more business (Grizzle & Sloan, 2016). Knowing the difference between mission creep and scope is important because resolving scope creep simply requires accounting for costs. Business leaders must identify mission creep or risk consequences to the company.

Mission creep takes place when a corporation has a lack of strategic focus (Grizzle & Sloan, 2016). The lack of focus emerges when an organization pursues too many opportunities that stray a company's operation away from its core competency. Essentially the business operates as a different company under the same corporate structure (Sarin, 2014). Companies chase their primary customer for their primary revenue. Business leaders pursue other business interests with their primary customer because they want to satisfy their best customer (Solomon, 2012). Firms also stray away from their core competency when pursuing revenue with other customers. Other customers offer compensation for similar services and products while the overall new venture can lead an organization to stray away from their long-term goals (Fader, 2012). Eventually, the company can lose their identity in the marketplace. The company may be able to recall their original company mission but often find themselves headed in an uncertain direction (Downes & Nunes, 2013). Often younger organizations discover the challenge to redirect their current business path to the original alignment of their long-term strategic goals.

B2B Branding

Providing a service is one of the oldest forms of trade. Services companies operate in a peer to peer business relationship (Peng, 2017). In a peer-to-peer business relationship, the service provider is visible to the client. This type of business relationship makes the service provider accountable for the level of quality of the services they provide to the customer (Hemel, 2016). The service level provided helps to build a reputation for the service provider. The reputation of the service provider becomes their brand. In a peer-to-peer business relationship, the service providers name is only as strong as its reputation (Ryan & Silvanto, 2013). Holistically, a service provider's reputation is important to business continuity and long-term sustainability.

Corporate Mimicry

People are flattered or annoyed when imitated and view the imitation is mockery (Dahl, 2014). In a marketplace, imitation is a common way of doing business. Corporate mimicry can cause a convergence in a market between the market leaders and the companies with the lesser market share (Andrzejewski, Hill, Grewal, & Puccinelli, 2016). Smaller companies mimic the business actions of the larger companies who lead their respective markets. This form of imitation develops sales for companies that do not lead in their marketplace (White & Argo, 2014). The companies start to mimic competitors risk losing their corporate identity.

However, this mimicry often limits companies by eventually taking the operations on a different strategic path. The company's identity ceases to align with original business goals and appear more like the goals of the market leaders (Ross & Sharapov, 2015). Although such a marketing plan may benefit the bottom line for a little while, a study by Brass (2012) indicated that corporate mimicry confuses customers. Organizations cannot strengthen their client base by starting their business with a strict business mission and eventually mimicking market leaders (Eyster & Rabin, 2014). Their services or products may appear to be competing however to customers and their needs, the services or products may look the same. Mimicry may be another reason why growing companies, and mature businesses venturing outside of their core capabilities, stray and encounter mission creep (Polidoro & Theeke, 2012).

Brand Trust and Credibility

Poor business leadership can lead to companies losing trust of their customers (Upamannyu et al., 2015). Companies that lose their customer trust also lose credibility among their peers in the market (Mishra & Choudhury, 2013). The loss of credibility gives a company's competitors a marketing edge. Competitors do not hesitate to expose weaknesses of other companies in their respective market (Tsai, Joe, Lin, Chiu, & Shen, 2015). When market leaders do not focus on their core competency, the company loses the lead in their respective market. The company loses a competitive advantage, creating financial vulnerabilities. When a company's client base no longer recognizes an organization due to a drastic change in capabilities, a lack of trust and loss of credibility takes place (Singh, 2015).

Customers become familiar with the company's level quality through word-of-mouth or direct experience with their respective service or product. The client's familiarity with the enterprise connects to its corporate image (Robertson & Arachchige, 2015). A corporate image is how a company looks to the outside world. Especially how a company looks to its customers and its competitors in its respective market. A good corporate image is critical to building brand trust (Solomon, 2012). Brand trust builds consistent and persistent brand imaging. A lack of brand trust may occur through poor execution of brand extension. Expanding a company's brand reputation is an unexpected risk to businesses that are still in its infancy stage (Robertson & Khatibi, 2012). Small businesses risk financial collapse if they cannot grow or transition due to an image problem.

Companies do a poor job expanding their brand or making reckless changes to their brand image risk a loss of trust with their core client base (Dubey, 2014). Similar to a service provider's reputation, a company's trust is impossible to regain if lost. Many studies exist on the topic of building brand trust, but little research is available on how to restore brand trust once squandered (Zdravkovic & Till, 2012). Business leaders need to take adequate care of their corporate image. The leaders of the respective organization are responsible for ensuring awareness of their respective corporate image within their organizations (Sushil, 2015).

Findings

Change within a corporation can happen in different ways (Mitchell, 2013). A company's response to change can determine their ability to withstand risk or turn the threat into an opportunity. Organizations need to respond to change by identifying the needs to improve capabilities to address dynamic environments (Pollack, 2012). Adopting a strategy like dynamic capabilities into an organization's strategic management plan can help companies to manage change without risk to their corporate identities (Mitchell, 2013).

Dynamic capability is a conceptual framework that companies use to adapt, create, and reinstitute organizational competencies to meet growing needs of their respective market (Teece, 2012). The dynamic capability extends a point of view that reviews the complexity to pursue different corporate capabilities (Eggers & Kaplan, 2013). The perspective establishes a valuation that measures the feasibility of mimicry and the company's ability to sustain market brand refreshment (Castiaux, 2012). A growing company's attraction to the changing environment is certain. The dynamic capabilities concept measures the managerial motivation against the corporate resources and time involved to create the evolution of capabilities (Helfat & Martin, 2015). Entrepreneurs and managers who can adopt a dynamic capabilities framework may be able to manage the growing competencies for their organization (Teece, 2012).

Focus on Your Best Customer

Just because a company thrives on change, for whatever reason, does not guarantee success. Changes in capabilities may decrease a company's performance in their respective market. According to researchers, companies should always focus on their best customer (Mitchell, 2013). Customer centricity describes an organization's focus on their best customer (Fader, 2012). The term *customer centricity* provides a basic rule of small business marketing and is essential for a strategic advantage. As a fundamental strategy, the purpose of customer centricity is to align its offerings with the needs of its most valuable customer (Fader, 2012). The goal is to extend long-term profits. Customers receive priority, and it is good business practice for companies to cater to their best customers (Cespedes, Dougherty, & Skinner, 2013). Even though the company may experience change or change their strategic direction to respond to market changes, the organizations should take caution when it comes to handling their best customers. Once a business loses a customer, recovering a lost customer is challenging and expensive to lure them back into doing business with you (Rawson, Duncan, & Jones, 2013).

Companies focus on their best customer but cannot seem to respond to the growing need to change. Businesses that ignore change become vulnerable to disruptive innovation (Pollack, 2012). Disruptive innovation is a management theory that defines how small organizations overtake large organizations (Hwang & Christensen, 2008). A small company surpasses a large corporation because the large company focuses on their best revenue and do not have the interests or resources to address the vulnerabilities presented by the small business (Cortez, 2014). The large company does not see the small company as a threat at first. By the time the large company addresses the disruptive company, it is too late for the larger organization to neutralize the disruptive threat. Big companies incorporate disruptive innovation strategies into their organizational change in strategic management goals as a response to addressing disruptive companies (Osiyevskyy & Dewald, 2015).

In response to disruptive innovation, companies have developed various mergers and acquisition strategies (Cortez, 2014). The responses consist of acquiring the small disruptive organization or funding a startup to compete with the disruptive target. Corporations purchase a shelf operation to shorten the time of market penetration and entry (Feldman, 2012). The purpose of the shelf corporation is to have an established legal formation. On paper, the company appears aged when actually the company's operations started when the acquiring corporation first confirmed interest in launching a new endeavor. Acquiring a shelf corporation is a solution that allows companies to react more swiftly to changes and threats in the marketplace (Muhammaddun Mohamed & Ahmad, 2012). Customer centric market incumbents possess the ability to mitigate disruptive threats by acquiring an aged legal formation.

Addressing changes in the marketplace can be costly (Mitchell, 2013). Not all companies have the available resources to address change (McKay, Kuntz, & Näswall, 2013). Financing may be a constraint to the company's ability to respond to changes. Obtaining small business funding addresses a company's need to respond to threats and vulnerabilities without any risky commitments of traditional bank loans. Companies may be able to finance their operations using invoice factoring in other special funding that requires collateralizing the company's receivables (Salaberrios, 2016).

Direction Change Planning

Corporations that successfully change capabilities have one primary attribute. Business leaders can see the need for change in advance (Eggers & Kaplan, 2013). Small businesses can successfully transform their business practices and policies to meet a rapidly changing environment. Research by Beske (2012) indicated that successful implementation of a change management system can help organizations to gain competitive advantages. Effective change management can help leaders address increasingly diverse market places and chaotic environments. In contrast, companies may experience dramatic and unpredictable changes (Helfat & Martin, 2015). A change management system consists of processes to help organize a fast and professional response unexpected and sudden change to avoid inevitable catastrophe. The procedures also include addressing workforce, supply chain, and stakeholder's resistance to change (Beske, 2012).

Conclusion

Companies should establish a robust change management plan. Organizational leaders should be able to identify disruptive competitors and develop an action plan. Action plans can consist of mergers and acquisitions, as well as induce special financing options to avoid risks to the core organization. A value exists to keeping to one's core competency. Companies should always identify their competition and document a plan to respond to threats in case the organization requires dramatic changes in business. Small business leaders should be able to determine mission creep and when it occurs. Focusing on the best customers is a good basic practice. Implementation of a dynamic capabilities framework into an organization's strategic plan helps to manage corporate change. Deviations in an organization's capabilities tend to confuse their customer base. Established brand trust and communicate changes to one's market identity to customers. Unplanned changes in capabilities diminish a corporation's identification and its respective market. However, a corporation's inability to grow and respond to rapid changing environments may result in business failure. Business leaders should use refractive thinking to address the changing competitive landscape and still maintain a good brand reputation by keeping the company's identity intact.

THOUGHTS FROM THE ACADEMIC ENTREPRENEUR

The problem to be solved:

- Entrepreneurs establishing and maintaining a long-term identity for their company.
- Preventing mission creep by proactively responding to market demands.

The goals:

- Understanding decisions company leaders make to confuse their customers by performing outside of their core competency.
- Understanding how dynamic capabilities framework may help companies to manage a market response.

The questions to ask:

- How can a company avoid diminishing their corporate image?
- How does a company effectively expand capabilities and retain customer loyalty?

Today's Business Application:

- Effective entrepreneurs adjust their short-term goals to remain aligned with their long-term strategy
- Consistent communication with customers can offset unnecessary confusion and promote buy-in from long standing client base.
- Change can be good and identity changes can be positive.

REFERENCES

Andrzejewski, S., Hill, K., Grewal, D., & Puccinelli, N. (2016). Should I copy her?: A meta-analytic synthesis of mimicry effects. *Advances in Consumer Research, 44,* 717-717. Retrieved from http://www.acrweb.org

Beske, P. (2012). Dynamic capabilities and sustainable supply chain management. *International Journal of Physical Distribution & Logistics Management, 42,* 372-387. doi:10.1108/09600031211231344

Bischoff, C., & Wood, G. (2013). Micro and small enterprises and employment creation: A case study of manufacturing micro and small enterprises in South Africa. *Development Southern Africa, 30,* 564-579. doi:10.1080/03768 35X.2013.817303

Castiaux, A. (2012). Developing dynamic capabilities to meet sustainable development challenges. *International Journal of Innovation Management, 16,* 1240013. doi:10.1142/S1363919612400130

Cespedes, F. V., Dougherty, J. P., & Skinner III, B. S. (2013). How to identify the best customers for your business. *MIT Sloan Management Review, 54*(2), 53. Retrieved from: http://sloanreview.mit.edu/files/2012/12/a2a8f8c8a7.pdf

Chen, Y.C., Chi, S.-C. S., & Friedman, R. (2013). Do more hats bring more benefits? Exploring the impact of dual organizational identification on work-related attitudes and performance. *Journal of Occupational & Organizational Psychology, 86,* 417-434. doi:10.1111/joop.12017

Hwang, J., & Christensen, C. M. (2008). Disruptive innovation in health care delivery: A framework for business-model innovation. *Health Affairs, 27,* 1329-1335. doi:10.1377/hlthaff.27.5.1329

Cortez, N. (2014). Regulating disruptive innovation. *Berkeley Technology Law Journal, 29,* 175. doi:10.2139/ssrn.2436065

Dahl, D. (2014). Social influence and consumer behavior. *Journal of Consumer Research,* S1-S2. doi:10.1086/670170

Downes, L., & Nunes, P. (2013). *Big bang disruption.* Retrieved from: https://ssrn.com/abstract=2709801

Dubey, J. (2014). Rebranding of Airtel: Did it work? *Journal of Marketing & Communication, 9*(3), 44-49. Retrieved from http://web.a.ebscohost.com.ezp.mywaldenalumni.com

Eggers, J., & Kaplan, S. (2013). Cognition and capabilities: A multi-level perspective. *Academy of Management Annals, 7*(1), 295-340. doi:10.1080/19416520.20 13.769318

Engelbrekt, K. (2015). Mission creep? The nontraditional security agenda of the G7/8 and the nascent role of the G-20. *Global Governance, 21,* 537-556. doi: 10.5555/1075-2846-21.4.537

Eyster, E., & Rabin, M. (2014). Extensive imitation is irrational and harmful. *Quarterly Journal of Economics, 129*, 1861-1898. doi:10.1093/qje/qju021

Fader, P. (2012). *Customer centricity: Focus on the right customers for strategic advantage:* Philadelphia, PA: Wharton Digital Press.

Feldman, D. N. (2012). Comments on seasoning of reverse merger companies before uplisting to National Securities Exchanges. *Harvard Business Law Review Online, 2*, 140-149. Retrieved from http://www.hblr.org/wp-content/uploads/2012/03/Feldman-Reverse-Mergers.pdf

Fischer, J. M. (2012). Responsibility and autonomy: the problem of mission creep. *Philosophical Issues, 22*(1), 165-184. doi:10.1111/j.1533-6077.2012.00223.x

Galia, R. (2015). The transformed identity of a banking corporation's employees, 1960s-1980s. *Journal of Public Affairs, 14723891*, 316-330. doi:10.1002/pa.1549

Goel, P., & Ramesh, R. S. (2016). An empirical study of the extent of ethical business practices in selected industries in India. *IUP Journal of Corporate Governance, 15*(1), 46-66. Retrieved from https://ssrn.com/abstract=2772515

Goldstein, H., Bergman, E., & Maier, G. (2013). University mission creep?: Comparing EU and US faculty views of university involvement in regional economic development and commercialization. *Annals of Regional Science, 50*, 453-477. doi:10.1007/s00168-012-0513-5

Grizzle, C., & Sloan, M. F. (2016). Assessing changing accountability structures created by emerging equity markets in the nonprofit sector. *Public Administration Quarterly, 40*, 387-408. Retrieved from https://paq.spaef.org

Hautz, J., Mayer, M. C. J., & Stadler, C. (2013). Ownership identity and concentration: A study of their joint impact on corporate diversification. *British Journal of Management, 24*(1), 102-126. doi:10.1111/j.1467-8551.2011.00792.x

Heesacker, M. (2005). Jack of all trades, master of none?: An alternative to clinical psychology's market-driven mission creep. *Journal of Clinical Psychology, 61*, 1067-1070. doi:10.1002/jclp.20138

Helfat, C. E., & Martin, J. A. (2015). Dynamic managerial capabilities: Review and assessment of managerial impact on strategic change. *Journal of Management, 41*, 1281-1312. doi/10.1177/0149206314561301

Hemel, C. (2016). *How to overcome the challenges of aligning the external image and the internal corporate identity when serving multiple market segments* (Master thesis). Retrieved from http://essay.utwente.nl/69158.

Jahromi, A. T., Stakhovych, S., & Ewing, M. (2014). Managing B2B customer churn, retention and profitability. *Industrial Marketing Management, 43*, 1258-1268. doi:10.1016/j.indmarman.2014.06.016

Lin, S., & Piercy, N. (2012). New product development competencies and capabilities. *Journal of General Management, 38*(2), 61-77. doi:10.1177/030630701203800204

Mazodier, M., & Merunka, D. (2012). Achieving brand loyalty through sponsorship: The role of fit and self-congruity. *Journal of the Academy of Marketing Science, 40,* 807-820. doi:10.1007/s11747-011-0285-y

McKay, K., Kuntz, J. R., & Näswall, K. (2013). The effect of affective commitment, communication and participation on resistance to change: The role of change readiness. *New Zealand Journal of Psychology, 42*(2) 29-40. Retrieved from: http://www.psychology.org.nz/wp-content/uploads/Kuntz1.pdf

Mishra, M. K., & Choudhury, D. (2013). The effect of repositioning on brand personality: An empirical study on blackberry mobile phones. *IUP Journal of Brand Management, 10*(2), 64-82. Retrieved from https://ssrn.com/abstract=2345205

Mitchell, G. (2013). Selecting the best theory to implement planned change: Improving the workplace requires staff to be involved and innovations to be maintained. Gary Mitchell discusses the theories that can help achieve this. *Nursing Management, 20*(1), 32-37. doi:10.7748/nm2013.04.20.1.32.e1013

Muhammaddun Mohamed, Z., & Ahmad, K. (2012). Investigation and prosecution of money laundering cases in Malaysia. *Journal of Money Laundering Control, 15,* 421-429. doi:10.1108/13685201211266006

Osiyevskyy, O., & Dewald, J. (2015). Explorative versus exploitative business model change: The cognitive antecedents of firmlevel responses to disruptive innovation. *Strategic Entrepreneurship Journal, 9*(1), 58-78. doi: 10.1002/sej.1192

Peng, F. (2017). *Investigation of online branding in B2B context in China* (Master thesis). Retrieved from https://aaltodoc.aalto.fi

Polidoro Jr, F., & Theeke, M. (2012). Getting competition down to a science: The effects of technological competition on firms' scientific publications. *Organization Science, 23,* 1135-1153. doi:10.1287/orsc.1110.0684

Pollack, J. (2012). Transferring knowledge about knowledge management: Implementation of a complex organisational change programme. *International Journal of Project Management, 30,* 877-886. doi:10.1016/j.ijproman.2012.04.001

Preechanont, P., & Tao, L. U. (2013). A comparative study of small business owner-managers' identity construction in b2b relationship marketing and business networking discourse in the UK and China. *Journal of Enterprising Culture, 21,* 495-532. doi:10.1142/S0218495813400049

Rawson, A., Duncan, E., & Jones, C. (2013). The truth about customer experience. *Harvard Business Review, 91*(9), 90-98. Retrieved from https://hbr.org

Robertson, A., & Arachchige, B. J. H. (2015). Identity of organizations: An analytical model. *IUP Journal of Brand Management, 12*(4), 7-38. Retrieved from https://papers.ssrn.com

Robertson, A., & Khatibi, A. (2012). By design or by default: Creating the employer identity. *IUP Journal of Brand Management, 9*(4), 31-47. Retrieved from https://papers.ssrn.com

Ross, J.M., & Sharapov, D. (2015). When the leader follows: Avoiding dethronement through imitation. *Academy of Management Journal, 58,* 658-679. doi:10.5465/amj.2013.1105

Ryan, J., & Silvanto, S. (2013). The critical role of corporate brand equity in B2B marketing: An example and analysis. *The Marketing Review, 13*(1), 38-49. doi:10.1362/146934713X13590250137745

Salaberrios, I. J. (2016). *The effects of using invoice factoring to fund a small business.* Retrieved from http://pqdtopen.proquest.com/doc/1761840902.html?FMT=ABS

Sarin, S. (2014). Relevance and creation of strong brands for B2B markets. *Vikalpa: The Journal for Decision Makers, 39*(4), 91-100. Retrieved from http://www.vikalpa.com/pdf/articles/2014/vol-34-4-91-100.pdf

Schuttler, R., & Lentz, C. (2013). Grieving, learning, and growing. A mentoring model for organizational and personal growth. *Journal of Psychological Issues in Organizational Culture, 4*(1), 100-108. doi:10.1002/jpoc.21086

Singh, R. (2015). Poor markets: Perspectives from the base of the pyramid. *Decision (0304-0941), 42,* 463-466. doi:10.1007/s40622-015-0114-0

Solomon, S. (2012). Finding a unified identity. How one health system's brand positioning came together after nearly three decades. *Marketing Health Services, 32*(3), 26-27. Retrieved from http://europepmc.org

Spady, J. G., & Kweli, T. (2006). The fluoroscope of Brooklyn hip hop: Talib Kweli in conversation. *Callaloo, 29,* 993-1011. doi:10/1353/cal.2006.0157

Srivastava, M., & Rai, A. (2014). An investigation into service quality-customer loyalty relationship: The moderating influences. *Decision, 41*(1), 11-31. doi:10.1007/s40622-014-0025-5

Sushil. (2015). Strategic flexibility: The evolving paradigm of strategic management. *Global Journal of Flexible Systems Management, 16*(2), 113-114. doi:10.1007/s40171-015-0095-z

Teece, D. J. (2012). Dynamic capabilities: Routines versus entrepreneurial action. *Journal of Management Studies, 49,* 1395-1401. doi:10.1111/j.1467-6486.2012.01080.x

Thakurta, R. (2013). Impact of scope creep on software project quality. *Vilakshan: The XIMB Journal of Management, 10*(1). Retrieved from http://www.xub.edu.in/pdf/Vilakshan-Sample-Article.pdf

Tsai, Y. H., Joe, S.-W., Lin, C. P., Chiu, C. K., & Shen, K. T. (2015). Exploring corporate citizenship and purchase intention: Mediating effects of brand trust and corporate identification. *Business Ethics: A European Review, 24,* 361-377. doi:10.1111/beer.12073

Upamannyu, N. K., Sankpal, S., & Gupta, M. (2015). Effect of corporate image on brand trust and brand affect. *BVIMR Management Edge, 8*(1), 28-41. Retrieved from http://ijas.org.uk

Walsh, G., Evanschitzky, H., Schaarschmidt, M., Walgenbach, P., & Beatty, S. E. (2016). Why B2B firms measure service productivity. *Rediscovering the Essentiality of Marketing.* doi:10.1007/978-3-319-29877-1_158

Wan, W. P., Chen, H. S., & Yiu, D. W. (2015). Organizational image, identity, and international divestment: A theoretical examination. *Global Strategy Journal, 5*(3), 205-222. doi:10.1002/gsj.1101

Webb, M. A. (2014). When and how to pursue corporate social responsibility with core competencies. *Business & Society Review (00453609), 119,* 417-434. doi:10.1111/basr.12039

White, K., & Argo, J. J. (2014). When imitation doesn't flatter: The role of consumer distinctiveness in responses to mimicry. *Journal of Consumer Research, 38,* 667-680. doi:10.1086/660187

Wiersema, F. (2013). The B2B agenda: The current state of B2B marketing and a look ahead. *Industrial marketing Mangement, 42,* 470-488. doi:10.1016/j. indmarman.2013.02.015

Zdravkovic, S., & Till, B. D. (2012). Enhancing brand image via sponsorship. *International Journal of Advertising, 31*(1), 113-132. doi:10.2501/IJA-31-1-113-132

About the Author...

Dr. Ivan Salaberrios resides in Pickerington, Ohio. Dr. Ivan holds several accredited degrees; a Bachelor of Technical management Science (BS) in Management from DeVry University; a Master of Business Administration (MBA) from Keller Graduate School; and a Doctorate of Business Administration (DBA) from Walden University. Dr. Ivan also is a certified Project Management Professional (PMP) and Lean Six Sigma Black Belt Certified

Dr. Ivan is the CEO and founder of AIM Technical Consultants. His career in the telecommunications industry began as a field engineer working with AMPs Radio Equipment, where he obtained extensive experience in RF Engineering, Network Engineering and Project Management.

In 17 years, Dr. Ivan has grown AIM from a handful of engineers to one of the largest staffing and engineering firms focused exclusively in wireless telecom. This growth is largely attributable to Ivan's relationship-building skills, dedication to exceptional service delivery, and unwavering focus on continuous improvement.

Dr. Ivan is a Gulf War veteran, serving an enlistment term in the US Navy on the USS Yorktown CG-48. He was honorably discharged in 1992.

To reach Dr. Ivan Salaberrios for information on consulting or doctoral coaching, please e-mail: ivans@aimtechinc.com

About the Company...

AIM Technical Consultants has experienced significant wireless industry growth since opening for business in 1999. We attribute this proven track record to our ability to consistently deliver IT field management and wireless technology implementation, allowing our customers peace of mind. Add to that our dedication to providing the best technical and professional services in the industry and AIM Technical Consultant's commitment to positioning ourselves as the *go to* wireless industry service provider, and the results speak for themselves. AIM Technical provides services in IT and wireless telecommunications committed to delivering unparalleled Cloud Engineering life-cycle support to our demanding customers with specific IT and wireless telecommunication needs.

For more information, please contact email: office@aimtechnical.com phone: (614) 452-7735, website: https://www.aimtechnical.com/

CHAPTER 4

Workplace Resilience Relevance for the Entrepreneur

Dr. Rose Marie Whitcomb

The entrepreneur's venture into business should include immediate and long-term goals towards resilience. When seeking to create a resilient career, one important goal is a profitable workplace, financial or otherwise. Resilience in a workforce and workplace will demonstrate profit, and in turn success for the entrepreneur. Becoming a refractive thinker, prepared to think outside of the box historically defining business, may allow the entrepreneur to reap benefits that others may miss. The level of success attained by the entrepreneur may correlate with how far they venture from the limitations of previous thought on their field of interest. Thus, refractive thinking will likely lead to a resilient and profitable future.

A detailed examination of the concept of resilience should begin with a concrete definition. "Fundamentally resilience is understood as a positive adaptation, or the ability to maintain or regain mental health, despite experiencing adversity" (Herrman, Stewart, Diaz-Granados, Berger, Jackson, & Yuen, 2011, p. 258). If resilience develops as a result of facing and overcoming adversity with a positive outcome, then the individual who demonstrates success within the workplace despite significant challenge is worthy of study. In addition, Bonanno (2004) identified three areas that correlate with resilience: (a) commitment to finding a meaningful purpose in life, (b) belief in the ability to influence events, and (c) confidence in the fact that both positive and negative experiences can result in growth. These three pillars provide significant value in the development of success both for the individual entrepreneur and the workplace. The entrepreneur seeking to maintain and retain a resilient workforce will do well to nurture and support these constructs within their organizational structure. This chapter provides an overview of what is common among those who excel in the face of adversity and demonstrates resilience in the workplace.

Resilience Theory Overview

If resilience could be acquired through osmosis and did not require surviving challenge and trial, life would be easier. But without the experience of hardship, success is much less rewarding. Resilience is a byproduct of challenge that if not successfully resolved, has at least been admirably faced and endured. Victor Frankl, Nelson Mandela, Lance Armstrong, and Michael J. Fox are but a few individuals who reported being enhanced by their challenges (Feldman & Kravetz, 2014). Each expressed a belief that life without their unique challenge would not be their choice, even if they indeed had an opportunity to choose. Even when an experience of adversity appears insurmountable, individuals often in hindsight report to being defined by the challenges they faced (Frankl, 1959).

Resilience is demonstrated by individuals who not only endure, but actually succeed, when faced with workplace challenge. Does this mean that there is something missing in those who face similar adversity and become overwhelmed to the point of burn out and resignation? Ablett and Jones (2007) attempted to discover the essential determining factor that exists when two individuals in the same workplace, who experience exposure to the same stressor, result in one employee facing the challenge with success and the other with discouragement. The difference may not be the *stressor* but the *stressee*.

This direction of study should be of interest to the entrepreneur launching into a business arena that is likely to include change and challenge. Employing organizations benefit from the tenure of their workforce, and the wise employer will invest in the facilitation of coping skills and the enhancement of resilience in their employee base. Many researchers focus on the common factors identified as resilience in adults who demonstrate strength and recovery following challenging experiences and this direction of study provides promise for the workplace (Seligman, 2011). When the common traits in coping style in resilient employees can be identified and quantified, the opportunity then exists to enhance these skills and as a result, create a more successful workplace.

In addition to *resilience,* the term *hardiness* is often used in writings focused on the successful workplace (Maddi, 2009). Hardy individuals possess characteristics including (a) a sense of control over the future, (b) a sense of purpose, and (c) an attitude that identifies challenge as opportunity (Herrman et al., 2011). The workplace is an environment where an employee with a sense of purpose, as well as a willingness to engage challenge with optimism, is demonstrating hardiness. A hardy and resilient workforce in turn provides benefit to the bottom line: profit and success for the organization (Adams & Boehr, 1998). The following two directions for resilience research are particularly applicable to the entrepreneurial business leader. First, there are valuable lessons to be learned from the experience of individuals who face challenge in the workplace, and thrive with demonstrated employment accomplishment (Maddi, & Khoshaba, 2005). If demonstration of hardiness and resilience provide benefit to the individual (by remaining employed) and to their employer (by retaining the valuable employee), the wise entrepreneur will seek to facilitate this state within their business environment. In addition, when employees demonstrate resilience in the workplace this construct can be identified, measured and enhanced (Maddi & Khoshaba, 2005).

Entrepreneurial efforts, across a variety of industries, will find that business success links to a resilient workforce and enhancing resilience in the workplace will provide a positive return on investment (ROI) for the entrepreneur.

Identifying employee resilience in the workplace provides a valuable return on investment. In addition, the tenured employee may provide a model of successful coping in the face of adversity, and in turn a path towards better resource management. The ability to recruit, hire, enhance and retain individuals with the potential to demonstrate resilience in the face of workplace challenge will be of significant value to an employer (Seligman & Schulman, 1986.) Creating a process to enhance resilience skills is an important personal and professional goal for the entrepreneur striving to succeed individually and build an employee base that best meets the needs of their emerging business.

The personnel (payroll / benefit) budget is often the largest operating expense for an employer and when managed well, provides a significant cost saver for the employing organization (Armstrong-Stassen & Ursel, 2009). Hiring individuals with attributes that fit well into the organization, while facilitating potential career advancement, success and longevity, is a goal that motivates many human resource (HR) professionals. Identifying prior to the time of hire, the individual likely to stay employed and provide benefit to the company, is a lofty task. Successful entrepreneurs will recognize the value of the human factor in their business model.

Entrepreneurial leaders understand that retaining the employee who offers strength in the face of challenge, as well as innovation and resilience when confronted with adversity, demonstrates benefit that reaches farther than the individual accomplishment. Although everyone will undergo stress in the workplace, some will experience the consequences of challenge more severely than others. Individuals who face stress in the workplace with hardiness, and overcome adversity with resilience, possess attributes of particular value to the entrepreneur (Masten & Coatsworth, 1998). Business environments must seek to endure and succeed in the face of change and a resilient workforce can be instrumental in redefining an organization's culture by infusing optimism and success in the midst of challenge (Seligman, 2006).

Resilience develops because of effective coping in the face of adversity. Since 2009, resilience in the workplace remains as a focus of study likely to continue in the future (Seligman, 2011). Entrepreneurs represent the cutting edge of the future of business and will proactively initiate change in advance of, or in response to, economic, political and technological upheaval. Entrepreneurs with knowledge of resilience theory will have an improved likelihood of success in overcoming adversity in the workplace.

Workplace Resilience

Entrepreneurs may benefit from research based on traditional workforce populations. Facilitating success in the workplace motivates all HR professionals as they assess the best appropriation of benefits for the most valuable employees. Workplace improvement historically included goals of assisting to: a) cut costs, b) reduce or eliminate waste and c) build upon the value of the organization (Vansteenkiste et al., 2007). In this regard, management teams focused on the role of benefit packages for increasing job satisfaction and employee retention. This approach to improved productivity has emphasized the influence of the organization upon the employee: job design, access to training, information management, and work environment design (Birkland & Birkland, 2005). Although evidence indicated that the structural environment, benefits, and working conditions do result in a level of improvement in employee retention; of interest to the entrepreneur may be studies that demonstrate that *money* may not be the best motivator in facilitating resilience in the workplace (Biswes, 2002).

When entrepreneurs as employers are motivated to hire and retain the most talented and productive workforce, this challenge often includes the provision of enhanced salary and benefit package incentives. Research demonstrates that happy and content employees perform as the most productive in the workplace and this fact motivates employers to do their best to facilitate this state (Albrecht et al., 2009). But, if monetary rewards do not correlate consistently with reports of happiness in the employee, reconsideration of these historically utilized incentives may benefit the employer. Continuing to rely on the tradition of increasing monetary incentives, while also maintaining a narrow focus on removing adversity or challenge from the workplace, may be counter-productive to success. Entrepreneurs may want to explore incentives in their benefit packages based on research into the identified employee population's unique and self-assessed sense of *reward*. Viewing the workplace from this new perspective may benefit entrepreneurs as they seek to personally maintain the highest quality of life as well as recruit and retain the best employee for their company.

Significant amounts of time and money are invested in an effort to address the concerns of employees who report to being overwhelmed and dissatisfied with their work (Vansteenkiste et al., 2007). Employers work diligently to identify and diagnose the workplace challenge and find the best way to reduce or remove the identified stressor. Utilizing this lens to view the workforce makes sense when an employer's focus is directed towards preventing employee burnout, reduced productivity and turnover. A disgruntled employee is likely to have a negative impact on the workplace and the employing organization (Adams & Boehr, 1998). Maslach's (1982; 2001) studies confirmed that negative events and stressors in the workplace may be precursors to poor personal and professional outcomes, including burnout and turnover. Workplace resilience research allows the entrepreneur to approach the examination of occupational performance from a different lens, that of the refractive thinker. These studies focus attention on the individuals who do not burnout or resign in the face of adversity in the workplace, but instead cope, recover and thrive despite the challenges they face. Seligman (2011) proposed that a new frontier for occupational psychology is research examining recurrent exposure to adversity, as often takes place in the workplace, and the ongoing success of coping and recovery skills demonstrated in the resilient employee.

Workplace—Nursing

The experience of the entrepreneur, especially in the early days of start-up, will not only include adversity, but it is likely to be a reoccurring state. When the response to challenge is more than an effortless *bounce back* following exposure to adversity, but is instead exemplified as a process of working to achieve beyond the previous level of functioning, the construct of post traumatic growth has been demonstrated (Tedeschi & Calhoun, 2004). Caza's (2007) research with nurse mid-wives included a foundational belief that "it is not despite adversity, but because of the experience of adversity, that individuals emerge with new knowledge, skills and increased competence" (p. 41). Growth following significant challenge, including traumatic events, is a goal that will facilitate success for the entrepreneur.

Although, nursing careers most frequently are within the traditional workplace, much of the expanded roles for nursing professionals have ventured into independent and out of the box opportunities. Caza's (2007) work examined the construct of post traumatic growth in the field of nursing, specifically with nursing mid-wives. These nurse mid-wife participants experienced adversity within the workplace and were enhanced by the challenge. As a result, they performed at levels of competence not previously achieved. Following significant challenge these nurse mid-wives were found to have re-examined how they saw themselves as individuals, as well as their role within the employing organization. Following this re-examination, the experience of adversity within the workplace resulted in performance improvement and employee retention. Entrepreneur's will also face frequent opportunities for review and reassessment of challenge and the role adversity plays in moving forward to an improved outlook on the workplace.

Palliative care nurses also experience significant adversity and challenge in the workplace and they too represent a resilient population. Ablett and Jones (2007) found work in palliative care to be inherently stressful. These nursing professionals work with patients who often experience significant pain and suffering with limited options for relief and the prognosis in palliative care is end of life, which often results in conflict and questions as the patient reviews life experiences and purpose (Ablett & Jones, 2007). In addition, the majority of healthcare energy focuses on treatment and cure, where palliative care is distinctly different. Yet, despite the inherent challenges, palliative care staff show lower levels of psychological distress, less burnout and turnover than other areas of healthcare employees. Interviews with hospice nurses have demonstrated common and recurrent themes of resilience. In the ever-expanding field of nursing, mid-wives and palliative care providers set a course beyond and sometimes opposed, to traditional health care. Nurses in these areas of practice often demonstrate out of the box thinking as they seek to provide the highest quality of care, even though their path may be different from what has been historically considered the industry standard of care. Launching into new areas of care with motivation to face adversity and succeed as a result, is a clear demonstration of workplace resilience and this aligns well with the role of the entrepreneur.

Workplace—Military

Entrepreneurial thought, may expand upon, and benefit from, demonstrated resilience research in traditional and institutional settings. The most significant research on resilience to date may be Seligman's (2009, 2011) contribution to the development of the U.S. Army Comprehensive Soldier Fitness (CSF) Program. An all-encompassing project in research and application, the CSF includes two primary principles: resilience is a result of a variety of cognitive, behavioral, and psychological processes; resilience is a skill that can be acquired. The U.S. Army CSF 2011 Report includes a summary of the evidence of the effectiveness of the CSF program following implementation with 22,000 soldiers across eight combat teams. In addition, a longitudinal study including a control group is measuring the effectiveness of the program moving forward (Lester et al., 2011).

In summary, the CSF program design included master resilience trainers (MRTs) participating in a 10 day training course at the University of Pennsylvania. These trainers include the assignment to one of four combat teams. Four additional combat teams without MRT participation were included in the study and The Global Assessment Tool (GAT) was administered on three occasions over 15 months (Seligman, 2011). Primary findings are:

* Treatment groups (those with MRTs) exhibited significantly higher scores in resilience and psychological health than the control groups (those without MRTs). Resilience can be enhanced.

* MRT exposure had the greatest impact on the 18-24 year old population, significantly more than with older soldiers. Introduction of resilience training early in a career has the biggest impact on change. (Seligman, 2011).

Although military training seeks to prepare and repair soldiers from exposure to adversity, Seligman's (2011) focus on the enhancement of resilience in the individual, was a dramatic change in direction for the established army culture. The prevalence of the resilient soldier has proven to be much more common than previously recognized. Most importantly, CSF includes a foundational theory that resilience is an acquired skill and research has demonstrated consistently that this is indeed true (Lester et al., 2011).

Meichenbaum (2012) also conducted a comprehensive examination of the resilient characteristics of military personnel post deployment. This work demonstrated that exposure to trauma did not prevent hardiness and success in individuals, despite the magnitude of the challenge experienced. Characteristic themes identified in Meichenbaum's work with resilient individuals included: (a) an ability to create and sustain supportive positive relationships, (b) focused positive emotions utilized to offset negative emotions, (c) a task-oriented coping style adapted to the specific challenge, and (d) cognitive flexibility demonstrating an ability to change thinking patterns not productive to the situation (Meichenbaum, 2012).

Entrepreneurs seeking to create a model of resilience for both themselves and their employee base, will do well to study the data from the military community. With the post-conflict influx of veterans returning to the civilian workplace, resilience experience has been demonstrated beyond theory. Coping skills that provide successful outcomes within the military can also be utilized in the workplace. Entrepreneurs who are also military veterans may include exposure to the CSF programming and will likely utilize their previous resilience enhancing training in their new business ventures and this will have a positive return on investment.

Workplace—Insurance Industry

A career in the insurance industry exposes sales agents to negativity, rejection and repeated failure. Prior to Seligman and Schulman's (1986) study, the Life Insurance Marketing Research Association (LIMRA, 1983) reported that a substantial percentage of sales agents quit within their first 3 years. Seligman and Schulman found that insurance agents with a negative and pessimistic explanatory style had an increased likelihood to demonstrate helplessness when faced with challenge and adversity, both of which are common to the insurance industry. In addition, this research demonstrated a correlation between explanatory style, productivity and success within this population of insurance salesmen in this challenging work environment (Seligman & Schulman, 1986).

These findings provided motivation for change in the insurance industry. Experienced insurance agents with an identified optimistic explanatory style sold more than agents scoring lower on this construct. In addition to productivity, agents scoring higher on optimism in their explanatory style were less likely to quit than those with a negative explanatory style (Seligman & Schulman, 1986). Increasing sales and retaining quality employees resulted in significant profit for the insurance industry and this research provides insight for the entrepreneur seeking to create and sustain success in their future business model.

Implications of Findings

Many individuals value their work identity as an opportunity to display competence and skill, explore personal interests, and make contributions to their field. Others see their work role from a perspective focused primarily on monetary incentives, influencing others and creating a prestigious position within a workplace (Armstrong-Stassen & Ursel, 2009). The wise entrepreneur will invest time in self-examination exploring these categories of motivation for both themselves and their workforce.

Vansteenkiste et al. (2007) studied employee work values by examining the intrinsic work value orientation, including self-actualization and self-expression, as well as the extrinsic work value orientation focused on security and material acquisition. Examination of the intrinsic vs. extrinsic motivation of the employee provides valuable information to the employer seeking to create a workplace that recruits and retains individuals best suited to meet the needs of their organization. "Specifically, if materialistic goals occupy a more important place in the employee's work value configuration, they experience more negative and less positive job outcomes, and they are more likely to intend to leave their jobs" (Vansteenkiste et al., 2007, p. 258). Extrinsic rewards are less likely to meet the needs of employees who are motivated by autonomy, competence and a sense of relatedness to the organization. These insights are important as employers attempt to facilitate an employee's overall sense of job well-being. The entrepreneur should consider the value of acknowledging an intrinsic mind-set in addition to traditional extrinsic benefits.

Change, challenge, and adversity, as well as the variety of responses demonstrated by individuals when exposed to each, make up the daily functioning of the workplace. When an individual who places significant value on their work identity is challenged at work, they are likely to respond in creative and innovative ways (Maddi, 2005). A positive sense of work identity also contributes to hardiness and resilience, which results in retention, tenure, stability and productivity in the workplace (Maddi & Khoshaba, 2005). Folkman and Maskowitz (2000) found that positivity in an individual results in successful coping with ordinary, everyday tasks, and the workplace primarily includes *everyday tasks*. Resilience following adversity is the most frequent response to challenging stressors, and yet this may possibly be the least studied or understood perspective. As entrepreneurs step outside of the box of traditional business models to create innovative and challenging opportunities for themselves and their employees, expansive and refractive thinking will be the foundation of resilience in these workplaces. The entrepreneur who acknowledges that challenge, coping and resilience are all pieces of the puzzle demonstrating success, will be prepared to utilize this mindset as a model for the workplace.

Conclusion

Research in resilience demonstrated consistently that most individuals facing adversity and challenge experience a period of reduced functioning, depression and anxiety symptoms, prior to returning to the level of coping experienced prior to the event (McFarlane & Yehuda, 1996). Successful coping and recovery is likely when individuals are exposed to adversity, even at chronic levels, and this is consistent both inside and outside of the workplace. The wise entrepreneur will utilize the data demonstrating that positive reappraisal is the process individuals use to make sense of challenge in their lives, and this successful method of coping allows for endurance in the face of change and adversity. Creating a work environment that thrives in the face of challenge is key to personal success for the entrepreneur and to retaining tenured employees, as well as enhancing success for the workplace. Building a life, as well as a workplace of resilience, will assist the entrepreneur as he or she moves successfully from theory to practice, using a refractive thinking approach to offer the market place the benefits of resilience and hardiness.

THOUGHTS FROM THE ACADEMIC ENTREPRENEUR

The problem to be solved:

- Discovering the best way to assist the entrepreneur to assess and enhance resilience in the workplace.

- Empowering the entrepreneur to avoid burnout or resignation in the face of adversity, while allowing successful coping, recovery, and thriving despite the challenges experienced at work.

The goals:

- To educate the entrepreneur on the construct of resilience as it pertains to success in the workplace.

- To strengthen the entrepreneur's optimistic outlook and faith in the process of resilience.

The questions to ask:

- What qualities exist in individuals who not only endure, but actually succeed, when faced with work place challenge?

- Is there something missing in those who face similar adversity and become overwhelmed to the point of burn out and resignation?

- What is the determining factor when two individuals in the same workplace, experience exposure to the same stressor, with a result of one facing the challenge with success and the other with discouragement?

Today's Business Application:

- Change, challenge and adversity are constant states in business and the wise entrepreneur will utilize their knowledge of resilient business practices to create a successful outcome in the workplace.

- Entrepreneurs with a goal of longevity in their chosen business venture, will want to facilitate a direction of success in a future filled with purpose and optimism solidified in resilience.

REFERENCES

Ablett, J. R., & Jones, R. S. (2007, December 14). Resilience and well-being in palliative care staff: A qualitative study of hospice nurses' experience of work. *Psycho-Oncology, 16*, 733-740. doi:10.1002/pon.1130

Adams, G. A., & Boehr, T. A. (1998). Turnover and retirement: a comparison of their similarities and differences. *Personnel Psychology, 51*, 643-665. doi:10.1111/j.1744-6570.1988.tb00255.x

Albrecht, S. F., Johns, B. H., Mounsteven, J., & Olorunda, O. (2009). Working conditions as risk or resiliency factors for teachers of students with emotional and behavioral disabilities. *Psychology in the Schools, 46*, 1006-1022. doi:10.1002/pits20440

Armstrong-Stassen, M., & Ursel, N. D. (2009). Perceived organizational support, career satisfaction, and the retention of older workers. *Journal of Occupational and Organizational Psychology, 82*, 201-220. doi:10.1348/066317908x288838

Birkland, S. P., & Birkland, A. S. (2005). Integrating employee assistance services with organization development and health risk management: The State Government of Minnesota. *Journal of Workplace Behavioral Health, 20*, 325-350. doi:10.1300/J490v20n03_07

Bonanno, G. A. (2004). Loss, trauma, and human resilience: Have we underestimated the human capacity to thrive after extremely aversive events? *American Psychologist, 59*, 20-28. doi:10.1037/0003_066x.59.1.20

Caza, B. B. (2007). *Experiences of adversity at work: Toward an identity-based theory of resilience.* Unpublished manuscript, The University of Michigan. Retrieved from ProQuest Dissertations and Thesis Database. (UMI No. 1183179)

Covey, S. R., Merrill, A. R., & Merrill, R. R. (2003). *First things first.* New York NY: Free Press.

Feldman, D. B., & Kravetz, L. D. (2014). *Super survivors.* New York, NY: Harper Collins.

Frankl, V. E. (1959). *Man's search for meaning* (Revised ed.). New York, NY: Washington Square Press.

Herrman, H., Stewart, D. E., Diaz-Granados, N., Berger, E. L., Jackson, B., & Yuen, T. (2011). What is resilience? *La Revue Canadienne de Psychiatrie, 56*, 258-264. doi:10.1177/070674371105600504

Lester, P. B., Harms, P. D., Herian, M. N., Krasikova, D. V., & Beal, S. J. (2011, December). *The comprehensive soldier fitness program evaluation* (Annual Report). Washington, DC: Department of the Army.

Maddi, S. R. (2005). On hardiness and other pathways to resilience. *American Psychologist, 60*, 261-262. doi:10.1037/0003-066x.60.3.261

Maddi, S. R., & Khoshaba, D. M. (2005). *Resilience at work*. New York, NY: MJF Books.

McFarlane, A. C., & Yehuda, R. (1996). Resilience, vulnerability, and the course of posttraumatic reactions. *Traumatic Stress*, 155-181. doi:10.1016/0287-07x36.2.136

Meichenbaum, D. (2012). *Roadmap to resilience*. Bethel, CT: Institute Press.

Seligman, M. P. (2006). *Learned optimism how to change your mind and your life* (3rd ed.). New York, NY: Vintage Books.

Seligman, M. (2011). *Flourish*. New York, NY: Free Press.

Seligman, M. P., & Schulman, P. (1986). Explanatory style as a predictor of productivity and quitting among life insurance sales agents. *Journal of Personality and Social Psychology, 50*, 832-838. doi:10.1037/0022-3514.50.4.832

Tedeschi, R. G., & Calhoun, L. G. (1996). The post traumatic growth inventory: Measuring the positive legacy of trauma. *Journal of Traumatic Stress, 9*, 455-471. doi:10.1016/j.cpr.2006.01.008

Tedeschi, R. G., & Calhoun, L. G. (2004). Post traumatic growth: Conceptual foundations and empirical evidence. *Psychological Inquiry, 15*(1), 1-18. doi:10.2207/11532796501i1501_01

Vansteenkiste, M., Neyrinck, B., Niewmiec, C. P., Soenens, B., De Witte, H., & Van den Broeck, A. (2007). On the relations among work value orientations, psychological need satisfaction, and job outcomes: A self-determination theory approach. *Journal of Occupational and Organizational Psychology, 80*, 251-277. doi:10.1348/096317906x111024

About the Author...

Dr. Rose Whitcomb, PsyD, LPC, NCC, CEAP, SAP—As a Doctorate in Psychology, Licensed Professional Counselor (LPC) in the state of Missouri and Kansas, nationally recognized Certified Employee Assistance Professional (CEAP), Board Certified Counselor (NBCC) and Substance Abuse Professional (SAP), Dr. Rose maintains a lifetime of learning.

With more than 30 years in behavioral health, Dr. Rose developed programming for many organizations serving a variety of populations, including: intensive in-home family therapy with at risk youth, detention and drug court services for juveniles, hospital based social services and employee assistance. As an active member of EAPA, APA and ACA, Dr. Rose strives to remain current in research and program design as it pertains to the health, wellness and productivity of the employee, family and the employer.

Dr. Rose resides in Kansas City Missouri with her husband of 34 years and enjoys taking time to bask in the success of her adult children, as well as appreciating the new and ever-increasing joy of her first grandchild.

To reach Dr. Rose Whitcomb please email rosewkids@aol.com

CHAPTER 5

Conquering the Myths of the Easy E-Entrepreneur

Dr. Natalie Casale

Undertaking the role of an entrepreneur is no easy task. Dedication, motivation, determination, risk-taker, passion, vision, and confidence are a few traits a person should hold to pursue this venture. In 2014, the U.S. metropolitan areas experienced a 50.3% increase in startups, a 9.6% increase from the prior year (U.S. Consensus Bureau, 2016). In 2015, 80% of small businesses survived the first year, the highest percentage reported since 2006 (U.S. Small Business Administration [SBA], 2017). Half of these companies are predicted to survive 5 years based on business survival trends of prior years (SBA, 2017). The entrepreneur who understands the business strategies to be a successful entrepreneur may contribute to the increase in this percentage.

An e-business may seem more appealing to start than a brick and mortar business. To understand the e-entrepreneur, a few terms require definition. An e-business is a business that operates on the Internet (Chao, 2016). The terms *e-business* and *e-commerce* should not be used interchangeably. An e-commerce can be an e-business; however, an e-business may not necessarily be an e-commerce. Simple creating a business webpage on the Internet is an e-business (Chao, 2016). Selling and purchasing goods and services on this platform defines an e-commerce (Meira, Magalhaes, Pereira, & Peres, 2014).

There are several myths why people select an e-business as oppose to a brick and mortar business: (a) creating a website is inexpensive, (b) attracting customers on social media is easy, (c) possessing a solid technical background simplifies the creating and maintaining of the e-business, (d) majority e-entrepreneurs are stay at home moms, and (e) Millennials think solely e-business. Understanding what is truth and not a misconception, provides refractive thinking for the e-entrepreneur.

The focus of this chapter is to determine what strategies, skills, and knowledge an e-entrepreneur can use to overcome the myths of the easy e-business startup. The specific problem is to avoid developing business strategies based on these myths that could be persuasive, providing false hope of becoming an e-entrepreneur. Becoming an entrepreneur or e-entrepreneur is not an easy task; however, understanding strategies that will assist in developing a successful e-business will contribute to the economic growth and development of the country.

Who is the E-Entrepreneur?

Characteristics of the entrepreneur and e-entrepreneur are the same. The difference is the *e*-entrepreneur is running an *e-business* (Chung, Chao, Chen, & Lou, 2016). The e-entrepreneur can also have a brick and mortar business. The focus of this chapter is the strategies and skills needed to start an e-business specifically. A brick and mortar component can be added later. As an entrepreneur, the e-entrepreneur is self-employed and self-managed contributing to economic development; therefore, an at home business is not an employed person telecommuting for a company that is not his or her own (Di Domenico, Daniel, & Nunan, 2014).

Advancements in technology provide an opportunity to start a business solely online (Chao, 2016; Richards, Busch, & Bilgin, 2010). The dream of running a business at home or on the beach using a computer with an Internet connection is indeed a reality. The e-entrepreneur can create a new electronic business operated on the Internet while residing at home (DiDomenico et al., 2014).

Zhang (2014) concluded college students seeking education of e-business startups should investigate programs that include details of the technology, business, and environment components needed to start an e-business. Students want information regarding business models, market research and strategies, and product opportunity of the business component to consider selling products or services on a web-based application (Zhang, 2014). Zhang suggested each component and its parts add important skills and strategies the e-entrepreneur needs to implement and develop a successful e-business.

The e-entrepreneur will use innovative business concepts available because of the constant changes in technology (Chao, 2016; Richards et al., 2010). The evolution of the Internet and building websites includes a plethora of options to build an e-business (Chao, 2016). These advancements in technology provide many opportunities for a creative and innovative e-business (Chao, 2016). Because technology continues to change and improve, the e-entrepreneur should remain current with technical advancements that could improve the e-business (Chao, 2016). The e-entrepreneur may also want to stay informed of new technologies that could move the e-business into a new trend, potentially taking the lead of competition (Chao, 2016).

An e-entrepreneur can be referred to as a digital entrepreneur. The digital entrepreneur uses digital technologies to start an electronic business and manage that business as an electronic enterprise (Chung et al., 2016; Zhang, 2014). Digital technologies include networking (Internet and cloud computing) (Zhang, 2014), interfaces (computers, laptops, tablets, and mobile devices) (Chung et al., 2016), and communications (email, applications, and social media) (Zhang, 2014). The e-entrepreneur can use a variety of digital technologies to start an online business (Chung et al., 2016; Zhang, 2014).

The e-business may or may not be e-commerce, and potentially began as an online enterprise in the home (Chao, 2016; Meira et al., 2014). Commonly known e-businesses include Amazon, eBay, Etsy, Expedia, Facebook, LinkedIn, Netflix, TripAdvisor, Twitter, and Yahoo. Facebook, LinkedIn, and Twitter are not e-commerce; therefore, a transaction of sales does not occur. Popular e-commerce organizations include Amazon, Ballard Designs, L.L. Bean, and Road Runner Sports. Each of these companies started as an e-business (Pauwels & Neslin, 2015). Leaders of these organizations explored and implemented a brick and mortar location whether successful or in preliminary stages or operation (Pauwels & Neslin, 2015).

In the United States, e-commerce sales continue to increase since 2008 (U.S. Census Bureau News, 2017). E-commerce has three main branches: business-to-consumer (B2C), business-to-business (B2B), and consumer-to-consumer (C2C) (Meira at al., 2014). An e-entrepreneur is most likely a B2C e-commerce, establishing an online retail business (Meira et al., 2014). The U.S. Census Bureau (2017) reported that 86.6% of $386 trillion of U.S. retail sales were from an e-commerce site, in 2015. With the increase in online sales, starting an e-business could prove worth the idea, time, and investment.

The digital entrepreneur cannot assume once developing the webpage, customers will come and purchase products. Creed and Zutshi (2012) discussed the continuous improvement for e-entrepreneurs should focus on key activities review, revise, reconstruct, and reveal. Many refer to this process as the circle of learning. Unlike the entrepreneur, the e-entrepreneur should seek training and education to create innovative processes for the e-business (Creed & Zutshi, 2012).

Lower Startup Costs and Expenses

The myth of becoming a successful e-entrepreneur is the startup costs are significantly less than starting a brick and mortar business. The e-entrepreneur can potentially set up a webpage for free.

There are a plethora of options to add a shopping cart and collection of payments. The option selected will vary in cost.

The e-entrepreneur can be a person who is inspired to start a business at home. The Internet provides a simple to use platform to start an e-business. The e-entrepreneur avoids the plan and cost for a tangible location that may include rent or purchase of a building, cost of expenses (utilities), community regulations, and design of a store or office space. Daniel, Domenico, and Sharma (2015) confirmed an at home business is appealing to a new entrepreneur because of the small investment needed to create a startup on the Internet. For those who want a start a business with minor risks and experience as an entrepreneur are attracted to starting an e-business (Danial, Domenico, & Sharma, 2015).

Web-design companies and user-friendly applications are available to create an attractive website to sell a product or service. These website development options are free or range in price based on technical advancements and capabilities. The problem the e-entrepreneur could face is finding the right web design and interface that is simple to use based on his or her technical knowledge and fit the needs of the e-business. Time spent searching for the best digital technologies could become costlier than the expense of selecting the website platform and business applications.

Three main functions are needed to sell a product: promotion, place orders, and accept payments. Social media applications are a quick and no cost option to market the products. Twitter and Facebook do provide extra marketing tools for an additional cost. The e-entrepreneur can take advantage of these services if the e-business can use the visibility or reach out to customers who may have an interest in the product for sale. The webpage must be designed to place an order, preferably into a shopping cart. The e-entrepreneur can set up a PayPal account to create a recognizable and easy option for payments. PayPal and other services provide a low-cost option for accepting sales.

Online shopping has become significantly popular through the years. Globally, $1.61 billion dollars of retail products were sold online (Statista, n.d.). Successful companies with both brick and mortar and online sales include Walmart, Apple, and Staples. With people becoming more comfortable with online shopping, e-entrepreneurs can take advantage of this popular phenomenon.

Mack, Marie-Pierre, and Redican (2017) concluded entrepreneurs surveyed believed visibility of the business is the top primary use for the Internet, followed by collecting information, providing information, and selling a product. The population surveyed for the study included entrepreneurs in Phoenix, Arizona, an area ranked number one in the United States for the most startups (Mack et al., 2017). Because this study was quantitative, understanding why selling a product was the lowest choice was not determined.

Marketing on Social Media

The myth is an e-entrepreneur can use social media to successfully market to the global customer and the cost is free. The e-entrepreneur can reach out to domestic and global customers at home on the Internet using social media applications, such as Facebook, Twitter, YouTube, Instagram, Pinterest, and Snapchat. Each application creates easy to use marketing tools to reach out to potential customers. Mack et al. (2017) determined entrepreneurs use social media for marketing purposes as oppose to gathering information about customers and products sold. More than half surveyed use more than one social media application (Mack et al., 2017). Mack et al. posited an entrepreneur would benefit from using the Internet if he or she understands how to use the Internet and its tools to maximize the business. Entrepreneurs want to avoid the trap of creating social media business accounts that are not used. Inactivity could make the e-business appear slow or unappealing. The concept of the mobile shopper has become more popular; therefore, using social media to attract customers could be easier.

Nawi et al. (2017) suggested the adoption of using social media as a marketing tool for promoting an e-business will enhance the performance expectancy. Entrepreneurs are more likely to accept the risk and failures of using social media for marketing products (Nawi et al., 2017). The surveyed entrepreneurs' perception of risks, trusts, and enjoyment for customers were significantly high; therefore, suggesting the confidence and success of using social media as a marketing platform.

Marketing on social media does provide different benefits from marketing word-of-mouth (WOM); however, the e-entrepreneur may want to consider electronic word-of-mouth (EWOM). Do not confuse WOM with EWOM. WOM is traditional marketing, such as advertisements on newspapers, television, mail, and flyers. EWOM is spreading information on the Internet. Vinerean (2017) posited the advantage to marketing on social media because of the customer increase in the use of online shopping and social media posts. Because retail sales continue to increase in the United States (U.S. Census Bureau, 2017; U.S. Census Bureau News, 2017), the e-entrepreneur will want to use EWOM for marketing.

Zulfogar, Sohail, and Shahid (2016) conducted a case study of a woman who started an online cake business on Facebook. The e-entrepreneur baked the cakes in her home and delivered the cakes; therefore, maintaining local customers. What made this business successful was not the ability to start a business online but how the owner marketed her business using online tools; the business was unique, the logo was distinctive and impactful, and the packaging material was deigned to be impressive and attractive. The e-entrepreneur focused on the visual of the brand, not just the products sold (Zulfogar, Sohail, & Shahid, 2016).

Creating a blog is another option to promote and market a business. Blogging is not social media; however, is a tool marketing tool that can help stimulate consumer interests about a business and its products. The e-entrepreneur can post a discussion in a blog that will benefit the business. Hu, Liu, Tripathy, and Yao (2010) concluded blogging could capture the attention of the consumer and influence the consumer to pursue interests of the product or service discussed on the blog. Therefore, blogging stores information about the products, whereas, social media is used as a platform to engage customers about the product and other pertinent information to grow a business.

The Need to be a Technical Expert

The myth is a person with strong technical skills has the knowledge to create and maintain an e-business. Technology has many forms: hardware, software, networking, and data. Computers, mobile phones, and tablets are hardware that may be used to start an e-business. The software can include programming and applications. A technical background could give an e-entrepreneur the advantage of using the plethora of available technical sources and maintain an understanding of the latest technical trends. If the e-entrepreneur experiences issues with any of the technical devices, he or she may be able to resolve the issue without the need to hiring help.

A person lacking in technical knowledge and wants to start an at home Internet business, you can purchase user-friendly tools to get you started or use existing applications such as eBay, Etsy, Facebook, and Twitter (Kenny & Zysman, 2016). Once the Internet business is set up, the e-entrepreneur will need to maintain the existing technology and perhaps add advance technical features to improve the e-business. One can hire a company to create the Internet business, manage the business, and market the business.

Kenney and Zysman (2016) concluded how technologies are used and deployed could provide an advantage and inspiration to create new e-businesses. Advanced and new technologies provide the tools for entrepreneurs to be more innovative and competitive. This advantage is not needed to start the business; however, presents an opportunity for the e-entrepreneur to use his or her technical skills to advanced technical e-business. Companies, such as Uber and Airbnb, were designed based on advanced technologies.

Mack et al. (2017) concluded a difference in technical knowledge between men and female entrepreneurs. Mack et al. determined female entrepreneurs included a willingness to invest in technical expertise. Although spending is an option, the e-entrepreneur may want to explore a brick and mortar business.

For Women Only

The myth is a stay at home moms are the best candidate to start an e-business. The Internet created a platform to influence stay at home moms to create an at home business. Do these women have the business experience and knowledge to start an at home business? Are they intimidated by their men competitors, successors, relatives, or partners? A woman who decides to start an e-business can balance personal life and a career, and develop a sense of empowerment. A woman considers her business another child; therefore, has the time management skills to juggle the business and family. Women are likely to include family to participate in the business as they do with help in the house.

Most people can easily start naming men as successful e-entrepreneurs, such as Mark Zuckerberg (Facebook), Jeff Bezon (Amazon), David Karp (Tumblr), Peter Cashmore (Mashable), Travis Kalanick and Garrett Camp (Uber), and John Zimmer (Lyft). There are also a few recognizable women who started an online retail store. Sophia Amoruso developed her online store on eBay, Nasty Girl; and Katia Beauchamp and Hayley Barna created Birchbox, an online startup for proving beauty product samples.

Kamberidou (2013) discussed how women entrepreneurs are transforming the work culture and stimulating economic growth with transformational leadership skills. The studied women who seek digital entrepreneurship, can balance a career and family and are comfortable with using new technologies and social media for their business (Kamberidou, 2013). Kamberidou (2013) conclusions were different from Simon and Way (2015). Simon and Way (2015) studied e-business entrepreneurship of Millennials in the United States. According to Simon and Way (2015), women makes less money starting an at home business than men; however, more women start an e-business. The study did not conclude if these differences were based on care-takers of children, education, or existing pay gaps between men and women who start brick and mortar companies.

Millennials have the Experiences for E-Business Success

The myth is lived experiences of the person born in the Millennial generation have the skills to become successful e-entrepreneurs. Popular e-business Millennial entrepreneurs include Mark Zuckerberg, creator of Facebook; David Karp founded Tumblr; Jessica Alba started the Honest Company; Peter Cashmore developed Mashable; and John Zimmer started Lyft. According to Hackel (2016), Millennials have the mindset of a digital entrepreneur. Shared characteristics of Millennials include proficiency in technology, socially connected, multitaskers, seek instant gratification and recognition, ability to balance personal and work, expect flexibility in the workplace beyond the traditional nine to five work hours, team builders, transparent, and seek career advancements (DeVaney, 2015). Millennials are confident and risk-takers (Hackel, 2016), traits of an entrepreneur.

According to Lingelbach, Patino, and Pitta (2012), Millennials know how to market. Millennials think global; therefore, traditional marketing is not as valuable to consider. Millennials seek information on the Internet or social media as oppose to other generations that use the television.

Khor and Mapunda (2014) posited Millennial entrepreneurs are not driven to make money. Millennials enjoy working with others and focus on using the skills they are good at. Millennials have minimal cash; therefore, seek startups that have low cost investments (Khor & Mapunda, 2014). Possessing the knowledge of technology, passion to work hard at what they love, and seeking low cost startups, Millennials are perfect candidates to become successful e-entrepreneurs.

Discussion

The myth is true that creating an e-business can be inexpensive. Danial et al. (2015) confirmed creating a website for an e-business is appealing because of the low expense; however, as Mack et al. (2017) explained the purpose of an entrepreneur wanting to use the Internet is to create an alternative means of visibility for the brick and mortar business. Selling a product online was a significantly low priority.

The myth of attracting customers on social media is easy is not necessarily true or false. Zulfogar, Sohail, and Shahid (2016) proved to start an e-business as a Facebook page can be successful; however, Mack et al. (2017) and Nawi et al. (2017) suggested entrepreneurs use multiple social media applications for an alternative medium to successfully market the products. The use of social media can be easy if used properly and often. Nawi et al. confirmed entrepreneurs accept the risks and failures if promoting products on social media do not prove valuable to the business. Social media is an option to present a customer-friendly experience for those who are comfortable using social media applications. As online shopping continues to become popular and more acceptable option to purchase products, entrepreneurs will want to take advantage of EWOM (Vinerean, 2017).

The myth of possessing a solid technical background simplifies the creating and maintaining of the e-business is false. Kenney and Zysman (2016) concluded entrepreneurs with strong technical skills could create an e-business that is innovative, providing unique products to consumers. Existing applications such as eBay, Etsy, Facebook, and Twitter, provide a web-based platform to run an e-business that does not require a strong technical background (Kenney & Zysman, 2016). For e-entrepreneurs that want to develop beyond the expectations of the consumer have the technologies to do so; however, is not necessary to start a simple e-business. Interesting to note, Mack et al. (2017) posited women are not as technically knowledgeable as men; therefore, women are willing to hire technical expertise.

The myth that a majority e-entrepreneurs are stay at home moms is neither true nor false. Women have the option to balance personal and home responsibilities to consider an e-business startup (Kamberidou, 2013). Although women use their leadership and social media skills to start a digital business (Kamberidou, 2013), what remains of concern, Simon and Way (2015) concluded in their study, was that women e-entrepreneurs make less money than men.

The myth Millennials think solely e-business is true. Hackel (2016) posited Millennials are programmed to be entrepreneurs, are socially conscious, and are natural users of social media for marketing personal and professional interests. Millennials work hard and prefer low costs startups (Khor & Mapunda, 2014). Not all Millennials will be e-entrepreneurs; however, Millennials do have the lived experiences to be successful starting an e-business.

Conclusion

The characteristics and traits of the entrepreneur and e-entrepreneur are similar. Becoming an e-entrepreneur could be easier than starting a brick and mortar business or e-commerce business because starting an e-business is an inexpensive option. The e-entrepreneur does not need technical knowledge to start an e-business. There are several tools and services that are free or inexpensive. Social media tools, such as Facebook, Twitter, and Etsy, provide a platform to sell and accept payments for products. Social media also serves as a platform to marketing products; however, should be used consistently to be successful. Although the stay at home moms appear to be the best candidates to start an e-business, most female e-entrepreneurs make less money than men and are not strong or confident in technical skills to start an e-business. Millennials do have the lived experiences and knowledge to become successful e-entrepreneurs. Most have limited funds; therefore, they seek low-costs startups. Millennials do have an advantage of becoming successful e-entrepreneurs because of their natural abilities to use social media for marketing not just themselves, but their products. Understanding what is myth and what is truth will help a person who is ready to start what he or she believes to become an easy e-entrepreneur. The refractive thinker considers making good business decisions and strategies based on what is true to create a better chance of e-business success and contribution to economic growth.

THOUGHTS FROM THE ACADEMIC ENTREPRENEUR

The problem to be solved:

- What strategies, skills, and knowledge are needed to become a successful e-entrepreneur?

The goals:

- Understanding the strategies an e-entrepreneur can implement to start a successful e-business.

The questions to ask:

- Is becoming an e-entrepreneur is easy because the startup costs are minimal and social media provides a free and easy to use marketing platform?

- Does an e-entrepreneur need a technical background to run an e-business?

- Can stay at home moms become successful e-entrepreneurs?

- Are Millennials born to be e-entrepreneurs?

Today's Business Application:

- The e-entrepreneur can start a business with zero or minimal costs and little or no technical knowledge.

- Social media tools can help an e-business if used regularly.

- Women continue to struggle with equality of pay and confidence as an e-entrepreneur.

- Millennials do have the lived-experiences to succeed as an e-entrepreneur.

REFERENCES

Chao, K. (2016). E-services in e-business engineering. *Electronic Commerce Research and Applications, 16*(2016), 77-81. doi:10.1016/j.elerap.2015.10.004

Chung, C., Chao, L., Chen, C., & Lou, S. (2016). Evaluation of interactive website design indicators for e-entrepreneurs. *Sustainability, 8*(4), 1-21. doi:10.3390/su8040354

Creed, A., & Zutshi, A. (2012). The e-learning cycle and continuous improvement for e-entrepreneurs. *International Journal of E-Entrepreneurship and Innovation, 3*(3), 1-12. doi:10.4018/jeei.2012070101

Daniel, E. M., Domenico, M. D., & Sharma, S. (2015). Effectuation and home-based online business entrepreneurs. *International Small Business Journal, 33,* 799-823. doi:10.1177/0266242614534281

DeVaney, S. A. (2015). Understanding the Millennial generation. *Journal of Financial Service Professionals, 69*(6), 11-14. Retrieved from http://www.national.societyoffsp.org

Di Domenico, M., Daniel, E., & Nunan, D. (2014). 'Mental mobility' in the digital age: Entrepreneurs and the online home-based business. *New Technology, Work and Employment, 29*(3), 266-281. doi:10.1111/ntwe.12034

Hackel, E. (2016). Let's take the mystery out of training Millennials. *Professional Safety, 61*(5), 8. Retrieved from http://www.asse.org

Hu, N., Liu, L., Tripathy, A., & Yao, L. J. (2010). Value relevance of blog visibility. *Journal of Business Research, 64*(2), 1361-1368. doi:10.1016/j.jbusres.2010.12.025

Kamberidou, I. (2013). Women entrepreneurs: 'We cannot have change unless we have men in the room.' *Journal of Innovation and Entrepreneurship, 2*(1), 1-18. Retrieved from http://www.innovation-entrepreneurship.com

Kenney, M., & Zysman, J. (2016). The rise of the platform economy. *Issues in Science and Technology, 32*(3), 61-69. Retrieved from http://www.issues.org

Khor, P., & Mapunda, G. (2014). A phenomenological study of the lived experiences of the Generation X and Y entrepreneurs. *International Conference of Business Strategy and Organizational Behaviour Behavior (BizStrategy). Proceedings.* 6-15. doi:10.5176/2251-1970-IE14.04

Lingelbach, D., Patino, A., & Pitta, D. A. (2012). The emergence of marketing in Millennial new ventures. *Journal of Consumer Marketing, 29*(2), 136-145. doi:10.1108/07363761211206384

Mack, E. A., Marie-Pierre, L., and Redican, K. (2017). Entrepreneurs' use of Internet and social media applications. *Telecommunications Policy, 41*(2), 120-139. doi:10.1016/j.telpol.2016.12.001

Meira, D., Magalhaes, L., Pereira, F., & Peres, E. (2014). E-commerce: A brief historical and conceptual approach. *International Journal of Web Portals, 6*(3), 52-60. doi:10.4018/IJWP.2014070104

Nawi, N. A. B. M., Mamun, A. A., Nasir, N. A. B. M., Shokery, M. A. H., Raston, N. B. A., & Fazal, S. A. (2017). Acceptance and usage of social media as a platform among student entrepreneurs. *Journal of Small Business and Enterprise Development, 24,* 375-393. doi:10.1108/JSBED-09-2016-0136

Pauwels, K., & Neslin, S. A. (2015). Building with bricks and mortar: The revenue impact of stores in a multichannel environment. *Journal of Retailing, 91,* 1820197. doi:10.1016/j.retai.2015.02.001

Richards, D., Busch, P., & Bilgin, A. (2010). The role of creativity (and creative behavior) in identifying entrepreneurs. *International Journal of E-Entrepreneurship and Innovation, 1*(4), 36-54. doi:10.4018/978-1-61520-597-4.ch009

Simon, J., & Way, M. M. (2015). Working for home and the gender gap in earning for self-employed US Millennials. *Gender in Management, 30*(3), 206-224. doi:10.1108/GM-07-2014-0067

Statista. (n.d.). *Online-shopping and e-commerce worldwide: statistics and facts.* Retrieved from https://www.statista.com/topics/871/online-shopping/

U.S. Consensus Bureau (2016). *Measuring America: Startups and job creations in the United States.* https://www.census.gov/library/visualizations/2016/comm/ startups-jobs.html

U.S. Census Bureau (2017). *Data: 2015 e-commerce multi-sector data tables.* Retrieved from https://www.census.gov/data/tables/2015/econ/e-stats/2015-e-stats.html

U.S. Census Bureau News. (2017). *Quarterly retail e-commerce sales.* https:// www.census.gov/retail/mrts/www/data/pdf/ec_current.pdf

U.S. Small Business Administration (SBA). (2017). *Frequently asked questions.* Retrieved from http://www.sba.gov/advocacy/frequently-asked-questions -about-small-business

Vinerean, S. (2017). Importance of strategic social media marketing. *Expert Journal of Marketing, 5*(1), 28-35. Retrieved from http://marketing.expertjournals. com

Zhang, S. (2014). Successful Internet entrepreneurs don't have to be college dropouts: A model for nurturing college students to become successful Internet entrepreneurs. *International Journal of Information and Communication Technology Education, 10*(4), 53-69. doi:10.4018/ijicte.2014100105

Zulfigar, S., Sohail, K., & Qureshi, M. S. (2016). Sam's Cake Factory: A delectable journey of a woman entrepreneur. *Asian Journal of Management Cases, 13*(2), 67-81. doi:10.1177/0972820116653340

About the Author...

Dr. Natalie Casale resides in Little Silver, New Jersey. Dr. Natalie holds several accredited degrees: a Bachelor of Science (BS) in Information Technology from Kean University, a Master of Business Administration (MBA) in Accounting from Monmouth University, and a Doctorate of Management (DM) in Organizational Leadership from the University of Phoenix School of Advanced Studies. Dr. Natalie is a fulltime university professor and associate online chair with Berkeley College, and part-time faculty with the University of Phoenix and Walden University. Dr. Natalie serves as a dissertation mentor / chair and committee member.

Dr. Natalie is a member of the University of Phoenix Lambda Sigma Chapter of the International Business Honor Society, Delta Mu Delta (DMD). Dr. Natalie is a volunteer National and New Jersey State District Leader of the Human Society of the United States (HSUS) and recognized community leader in animal welfare.

To reach Dr. Natalie Casale, please visit her website: http://www.doctor nc15.com or e-mail: nataliecasale@mac.com

CHAPTER 6

Can Small Business Identify Unethical Business Behavior?

Dr. Karen J. Tillman

Unethical behavior by a few who work within various business markets have cost the American public an estimated $6.3 million (Report to the Nations, 2016). Businesses with less than 100 employees are more susceptible to employees displaying unethical behavior by 31.8% (Hrncir, Metts, & Smith, 2012). Researchers conducted studies on moral reasoning and ethical decision-making and the general impact on businesses (Bagdasarov, Harkrider, Johnson, Mumford, & Thiel, 2012; Jackson, Wood, & Zboja, 2013; Pendse, 2012; Zuber, 2015). However, comparatively few researchers focused on business related issues of the moral reasoning and ethical decision-making of IT employees who work for small businesses (Banerjee & Dutta, 2011). Consequently, business executives wasted billions of dollars in company money on unethical business acts (Schwartz, 2012).

A lack of morals and ethics by U.S. leaders and employees within many industries led to organizational failures (Bejou & Greenberg, 2012). According to Baker, Detert, Mayer, Moore, and Trevino (2012), unethical behavior by a few members of an organization can have a negative influence on the entire organization. The ability of an organization's leadership to gain the trust of employees becomes questionable when evidence of members within the organizations' acts of unethical behavior surfaces (Gove & Janney, 2011). As a result, such pervasive evidence of wrong acts caused

entrepreneurs to reassess the organization's present ethics policies. This study included examination of some Maryland metropolitan based entrepreneurs contracting with the Department of
Defense (DoD) and if ethics training (ET), education level (EL) and
employee's perception of their organizations' ethical leadership
(EP) predicted an IT employees' engagement in unethical business
behavior. Entrepreneurs need to shift their current way of thinking
to shift to refractive thinking approach when assessing the effectiveness of their ethical policies to measure whether there should
be a change in policy development. In this study small business and
entrepreneurship are intertwined.

Background

Business violations caused by employees often result in an intu-
itive, but disastrous ripple effect that moves from lost contracts
to lost jobs (Timofeyev, 2014). Entrepreneurs who use the refractive thinking approach can consider ways to identify and avoid
unethical business behavior. From January 2014 through October
2015, unethical business behavior caused small businesses to lose
on average $120,000 with a total impact in the billions of dollars
("Report to the Nations," 2016).

Methodology

To assist with the analysis of a theory, researchers use quantitative research (Leggett & Yates, 2016). The business problem
required an analysis of the numerical data to examine if a correlation exists between ET, EL, and EP. According to Lach (2014),
researchers use quantitative analysis to collect, analyze, and com-
pare data to test one or more hypotheses. The goal was to project
study findings across broader populations. The primary research
question (RQ) guiding this study was: Does ET, EL, and EP predict

the likelihood of Maryland metropolitan based IT employees' engagement in unethical business behavior?

The instruments for the research study consisted of two existing survey instruments augmented with a set of demographic questions. Harris (2000) developed the Ethics in IT instrument to include 22 vignettes related to the potential IT dilemmas. The data collected from the Ethics in IT survey provides insight into participant's ethical decision-making. The second survey instrument, the Defining Issues Test (DIT-2), devised by Rest in 1999, contain a set of five sample dilemma stories for the participants to read (Bailey, 2011). The DIT-2™ test provides the researcher with insight into the moral reasoning of the participant.

Using the theoretical framework aided with the structuring of the research problem, the research findings, the description of other studies, as well as who could benefit from the study (Bryman, 2012). The theoretical framework for this study included Kohlberg's (1958) moral development theory (as cited in Hersh & Kohlberg, 1977). In 1958, Kohlberg developed the moral development theory (MDT). According to Bhardwaj, Dhingra, Srivastava, and Srivastava (2013), Kohlberg's theory provides three levels of moral reasoning. The three levels identified were (a) a preconventional level (Stages 1 and 2), (b) a conventional level (Stages 3 and 4), and (c) a postconventional level (Stages 5 and 6) (as cited in Bhardwaj et al., 2013).

Ethical Problems in the Information Technology Profession

Computers and the Internet seem to open new challenges in the IT profession, specifically concerning computer privacy and security. In the IT field, IT professionals seem to have access to a good deal of information. IT and the potential access to information and uses can incite people to behave unethically (Buckley, Creese, Goldsmith, & Legg, 2015). Opportunity can also incite a person to behave unethically. In understanding the moral development theory, potential and opportunity develops during the moral motivation stage followed by moral judgment, which might assist a person in deciding what is morally correct.

Safeguards could be put in place that may cause a person to think about repercussions before acting on potential opportunities of unethical behavior. According to Davis, Powell, and Read (2014), solutions such as audits could help lessen the opportunity for employees to act unethically. Auditing tracks execution actions, by whom, and provides a timeline. Auditing makes people within an organization accountable for their actions. Chatterjee, Sarker, and Valacich (2015) conducted two empirical studies to test this theory. Chatterjee et al. provided examples of the type of social media technology people use, such as Facebook, online dating sites, Craigslist, and chat rooms misleadingly. Chatterjee et al. (2015) discussed misleading uses of IT, such as not representing oneself truthfully, collecting private identity information, spying on children, and stalking. According to Chatterjee et al., these unscrupulous acts instigated IT security breaches such as identity theft, denial of service, and cyber-attacks. Chatterjee et al. indicated that social, situational, and technological factors influence unethical behavior. Chatterjee et al. concluded that a lack of audit trails and traceability could contribute to employees in practicing unethical behavior.

People who practice unethical behavior have one thing in common: They feel untouchable, and many feel they are smarter than the law. Doyle, Lount, Pettit, and To (2015) and Gino, Moore, Ruedy, and Schweitzer (2014) concluded that people's moral reasoning led them to think that if they can get away with bad behavior such as stealing, they take the chance. Ahluwalia and Merhi (2014) went one step further and stated that the level of punishment also influences an employee's willingness to display unethical behavior. Gino (2015) agreed with the previous studies, adding that some individuals who hold high moral values are more likely to commit unethical behavior when the opportunity is present.

Ethics Training

Research on ethics training and the impact on moral reasoning and ethical decision-making of IT employees from small businesses is scarce. Skepticism exist concerning ethics training among scholars from previous research about ethical decision-making. According to Pitesa and Thau (2013), research on moral development, a person's interaction with the environment influences values and morals, therefore, influencing decision making. IT Employees in businesses must understand the values and morals, in which they acquire through the environment, may not align with the organization. Ethics training may be vital to workers making sound ethical decisions.

The results from studies on ethics training are a part of the investigation of the significance of ethics training on ethical decision-making. According to Wright (2013), a good business practice includes annual ethics training. However, according to Albrecht and Holland (2013), a lack of ethics training exists in small businesses. Researchers questioned if ethics training mattered in connection with ethical decision-making. According to researchers (Clements & Shawver, 2014; Gasper, Laufer, & Warren 2014; Luth, May, & Schwoerer, 2014), ethics training matter, especially when ethics training has an impact on an individual's decision-making.

According to a study performed by Birch, Tesfom, and Tessema (2013), ethics training did not matter and could not teach an individual to make good ethical decisions. Weber (2014) agreed with the previous research findings. According to Weber (2014), the ineffectiveness of ethics training stemmed from a lack of resources, trainers, insufficient budgets, and time allotted for training. Weber pointed out an increase for ethics training, as well as a need and a high demand over the recent years; however, the training lacked effectiveness.

Several researchers noted that if systematically taught ethical training could be effective in the business environment (Fryer, 2015; Gonzalez-Canton, Rohlfer, & Slocum, 2014). Fryer (2015), and Gonzalez-Canton et al. (2014) agreed on ethics training being important to the survival of an organization. Raile (2013) stated that continued ethics training raises the ethical perception of an organization; thereby influences positive change. Beeri, Dayan, Vigoda-Gadot, and Werner (2013) conducted a longitudinal study with 108 employees. Employees went through a yearlong ethics program within the organization. Information gathered from the yearlong program led Beeri et al. to conclude that the ethics program produced positive awareness concerning ethics, codes of ethics, and an upsurge in ethical decision-making.

The overall assumption from previous research on the topic may lead a researcher to believe that ethics training might aid in moral reasoning, thus impacting the ethical decision-making. Understanding the importance of ethics training adds credence to the impact ethics training may have on an employee's ethical decision-making.

Ethical Leadership

The role of effective leadership in a business environment created extensive research. According to Allen, Ericksen, and Collins (2013), leaders set the tone of a small business. This train of thought coxed researchers to believe that ethical leadership can affect an individual's moral reasoning and ethical decision-making.

Xinxin and Yidong (2013) conducted a multilevel analysis using questionnaires to test the theory on ethical leadership's influence on employees work behavior. The questionnaire included 302 employees from different areas of work within two different agencies. The results of the study led Xinxin and Yidong to conclude a direct correlation between employees work behavior and the employees' perception of ethical leadership.

According to Avella and Nunn (2015), ethical leadership not only has a direct correlation with employees making good ethical decisions, but could also lead to the company's success. The leadership within a business setting can inspire and nurture talents within an organization (Peters & Reveley, 2014). Leadership must be able to build trust, execute ethical standards, and inspire employees (Bottomley, Burgess, & Fox, 2014). Building trust and inspiring employees could lead to ethical decision-making by employees.

Ethical leadership could change an employees' business behavior. However, some researchers believe there is not enough research data to quantitatively back up this belief. Some researchers call for additional research between ethical leadership and employees' business behavior (Akdogan & Demirtas, 2015). However, De Hoogh, den Hartog, and Kalshoven (2013) stated that research on ethical leadership and its effects has increased in recent years. De Hoogh et al. goes on to explain that employees perceived ethical leadership within an organization depends on the employees' knowledge of *moral awareness*.

Unethical Decision-Making and Culture

Understanding a business culture can help to understand the moral reasoning. Consequently, this understanding of moral reasoning can lead to understanding the unethical decision-making by employees. The culture the leaders within an organization establishes could impact how employees feel. According to Pierce and Snyder (2015), the culture of the company could influence the ethical decision-making of its employees.

Dickerson, Festervand, and Vitell (2000) conducted a quantitative study to see if small businesses experience similar ethical problems as larger organizations. In searching for an answer concerning ethical behavior within a small business Dickerson et al. mailed surveys to 1,300 small businesses to gather data. Variables tested included (a) personal ethics, (b) business practices, (c) business standards, (d) stakeholder responsibility, and (e) response to unethical behavior (Dickerson et al., 2000). Small businesses, like other organizations, had employees who engaged in unethical behavior according to the research conducted by Dickerson et al. Through statistical analysis, Dickerson et al. demonstrated that supervisors set the tone for ethical behavior within businesses. The results of the study can assist researchers in gaining important knowledge in understanding ethical practices within businesses whether the business is small versus ethical practices within larger organizations. The results of the study can assist researchers in understanding how business standards and leadership affect the success of businesses.

Participants

To gain access to participants, this survey used snowball sampling. Snowball sampling is appropriate when a question exists regarding finding a large enough or hard to find sample size (Ardern, Nie, Perez, Radhu, & Ritvo, 2013; Arieli & Cohen, 2011; Heckathorn, 2011). The use of snowball sampling in this study ensured the study achieved a sample size sufficient to draw a valid conclusion. The use of snowball sampling was to receive recommendations for new participants and introductions to establish a professional relationship. Snowball sampling is the appropriate sampling method for this type of research because of the restricted and sensitive nature of the DoD. According to Fisher and Monahan (2015), snowball sampling is a good technique to use when trying to gain access to *private or secure* organizations.

Research Design

The research design for this study was correlational. The design included three independent variables and two dependent variables. Multiple regression analysis assisted with the examination on whether the three independent variables (as a set) were significantly related to moral reasoning and ethical decision-making. Correlational design can assist a researcher to explain if each variable separately supports in predicting decision-making independently of the outcome of the other variables. A correlational study was the most appropriate design for addressing the primary and subsidiary research questions.

Software tools such as G*power assist in calculating sample sizes for assuring statistical validity (Buchner et al., 2009). Using a medium sample size of 0.15 and power set to .80, the regression analysis required an approximate sample size of 68 for the study. The collection of a sample this size helps to ensure the significance is strong where it exist, and contributed to the validity of the study. Increasing the sample size to 107 increases the power to .95. Therefore, seeking a range of participants between 68 and 107 was the intent for the study.

The data collection method for the study was an online survey software tool through SurveyMonkey. SurveyMonkey is an online tool that aids researchers in collecting data (Chui, Sherry, & Thomas, 2010; Danitz & Orsillo, 2014; Jeston, McDonald, & Pollock, 2014). The Universal Resource Locator (URL) provided by SurveyMonkey provided each participant the ability to sign on to the survey through his or her email address. The link included background information and instructions on how to fill out the survey and the ability to exercise the option of not participating in the study.

The data were collected using the DIT-2 to test moral development and the Ethics in IT survey to test the ethical decision-making.

To test the moral development, the raw data collected were delivered via email to The Center for the Study of Ethical Development for tabulation where the P score and $N2$ score were calculated. The means, standard deviation, variances, and correlations were calculated using the data indexes and other data. Conducting a correlations test would reveal if a relationship exists between the variables.

To test ethical decision-making, the survey data collected from the Ethics in IT survey were coded, tabulated, and scored using SPSS software v21. All the scores were added for each of the survey participants to create an index. The index made the process easier to use the scores.

The assumptions of multicollinearity, outliers, normality, linearity, homoscedasticity, and independence of residuals were evaluated. Bootstrapping, using 2,000 samples, enabled combating the influence of assumption violations. The assumptions were met, and no serious violations were evident. Tests to understand if the data met the assumption of collinearity indicated no significant violation. The largest variance inflation factor was less than 10, and the average of the variance inflation factors was 1.02 and therefore not considered as substantially greater than one.

Calculating the correlation coefficient of the predictor variables detected no multicollinearity existed. The data met the assumption of independent errors Durbin-Watson value = 1.98. The results from the examination indicated no major violations of the assumptions. Normality, homoscedasticity, and linearity assumptions were tested using the normal probability P-P plot. The results displayed a normal distributed residual. The P-P plot is a display of the regression standardized residual, which showed data points that were not completely on the regression line, but within close proximity.

Forty-two out of 112 total returned surveys were eliminated because of missing data. Thus, 70 participants completed the survey and were included in the descriptive statistics. From 70 completed surveys, four did not meet the (CSED) reliability check;

therefore, these were taken out of the Ethics in IT Survey analysis. The average number of IT employees who participated in ET was 83%. The average education level was 46% holding a Master's degree, and employee's perception of their organizations' ethical leaders was 83%.

Standard multiple linear regression, [alpha] = .05 (two-tailed), was used to examine the efficacy of ET, EL, and EP in predicting employees' moral development and ethical decision-making. Preliminary analyses conducted to assess whether the assumptions of multicollinearity, outliers, normality, linearity, homoscedasticity, and independence of residuals were met; no serious violations were noted. The model was not able to significantly predict the likelihood of Maryland metropolitan based IT employees' engagement in unethical business behavior. This result showed an approximate 28% of variations in moral development and ethical decision-making is accounted for by the linear combination of the predictor variables (ET, EL, and EP). The ad hoc analysis of the relationship between moral development and ethics in IT findings displayed a significant relationship between Stage 2/3 personal interest and Stage 4 maintain norms moral development and ethical decision-making.

Kohlberg's (1958) Stage 2/3 personal interest indicates a person with a high score shows a high degree of societal conformism. At the Stage 4 level of Kohlberg's moral development theory, an individual has respect for authority and rules. The results of the consolidated scores revealed that most participants fell within the maintaining norms stage of moral reasoning.

Conclusion

Until now, little research on moral development and ethical decision-making focused on employees in information technology who worked for a small business. Most research studies on moral development and ethical decision-making centered on college students or professionals in the accounting field. This study adds additional knowledge that was lacking in the small business arena; thereby, adding value to the business environment in understanding if moral development and ethical decision-making assist in predicting which IT employees may display unethical behavior. The study results provide business managers, IT program managers, and human resource manager's awareness, that ET, EL, and the EP have no significant effect in predicting which IT employees may display unethical business behavior.

This research study has several limitations. Generalizability, participant pool, and the lack of prior studies in the DoD environment that examined the relationship between moral development and ethical decision-making of IT employees. The third limitation was the lack of prior studies in the DOD environment. Prior studies on moral development and ethical decision-making included only college students or professionals in the accounting field. Future researchers could use this study as a template for research on similar businesses to examine the relationship between moral development and ethical decision-making of IT employees. While, whistleblowing was not a part of this study, research results revealed that whistleblowing can affect an employees' ethical decision-making. Retaliation or dismissal from whistleblowing can have negative consequences on employees within an organization (Mayer, Nurmohamed, Schminke, Shapiro, & Trevino, 2013).

There is a lack of research in the small business community on moral development and ethical decision-making among IT employees in the business arena. Yet, unethical business behavior continues to inundate the front pages of major newspapers and news media. Media reports will continue to increase, unless new ways are discovered to recognize possible unethical intentions early; limit risk, thereby, possibly preventing bad behaviors.

THOUGHTS FROM THE ACADEMIC ENTREPRENEUR

The problem to be solved:

- Identify employees who may act unethically

The goals:

- Understanding the need to manage unethical business behavior
- Bringing awareness to entrepreneurs on the effects of unethical business behavior

The questions to ask:

- How can organizations effectively identify unethical behavior?
- Can identifying unethical dilemmas assist business managers to circumvent bad behavior and avoid contract losses?

Today's Business Application:

- Small businesses that understand unethical business behavior can be better prepared in identifying bad behavior.
- Small business owners can work towards preventing contract and job losses by implementing programs that address unethical business behavior.

REFERENCES

Ahluwalia, P., & Merhi, M. (2014). The role of punishment and task dissonance in information secuirty policies compliance. Retrieved from http://www.aisel.aisnet.org

Akdogan, A. A., & Demirtas, O. (2015). The effect of ethical leadership behavior on ethical climate, turnover intention, and affective commitment. *Journal of Business Ethics, 130*, 59-67. doi:10.1007/s10551-014-2196-6

Albrecht, C., & Holland, D. (2013). The worldwide academic field of business ethics: Scholars' perceptions of the most important issues. *Journal of Business Ethics, 117*, 777-788. doi:10.1007/s10551-013-1718-y

Allen, M. R., Ericksen, J., & Collins, C. J. (2013). Human resource management, employee exchange relationships, and performance in small businesses. *Human Resource Management, 52*, 153-173. doi:10.1002/hrm.21523

Ardern, C. I., Nie, J. X., Perez, D. F., Radhu, N., & Ritvo, P. (2013). Impact of participant incentives and direct and snowball sampling on survey response rate in an ethnically diverse community: Results from a pilot study of physical activity and the built environment. *Journal of Immigrant Minority Health, 15*, 207-214. doi:10.1007/s10903-011-9525-y

Arieli, T., & Cohen, N. (2011). Field research in conflict environments: Methodological challenges and snowball sampling. *Journal of Peace Research, 48*, 423-435. doi:10.1177/0022343311405698

Avella, J. T., & Nunn, S. G. (2015). Does moral leadership conflict with organizational innovation? *Journal of Leadership Studies, 9*, 85-87. doi:10.1002/jls.21417

Bagdasarov, Z., Harkrider, L., Johnson, F. J., Mumford, M. D., & Thiel, C. E. (2012). Leader ethical decision making in organizations: Strategies for sensemaking. *Journal of Business Ethics, 107*, 49-64. doi:10.1007/s10551-012-1299-1

Bailey, C. D. (2011). Does the defining issues test measure ethical judgment ability or political position? *Journal of Social Psychology, 151*, 314-330. doi:10.1080/00224545.2010.481690

Baker, V. L., Detert, J. R., Mayer, D. M., Moore, C., & Trevino, L. (2012). Why employees do bad things: Moral disengagement and unethical organizational. *Personnel Psychology, 65*, 1-48. doi:10.1111/j.1744-6570.2011.01237.x

Banerjee, S., & Dutta, S. (2011). Ethical practices towards employees in small enterprises: A quantitative index. *International Journal of Business Management & Economic Research, 2*, 205-221. Retrieved from http://www.ijbmer.com/

Bejou, D., & Greenberg, B. (2012). A call to corporate compassion. *Journal of Relationship Marketing, 11*, 1-6. doi:10.1080/15332667.2012.653602

Bhardwaj, A., Dhingra, V., Srivastava, A., & Srivastava, C. (2013). Morality and moral development: Traditional Hindu concepts. *Indian Journal of Psychiatry, 55,* 283-287. doi:10.4103/0019-5545.105552

Birch, N. J., Tesfom, G., & Tessema, M. T. (2013). Perceptions of real estate agents on the role of professional training in ethical decision making. *International Journal of Business Governance and Ethics, 8,* 348-375. doi:10.1504/IJBGE.2013.059168

Bottomley, K., Burgess, S., & Fox, M. III., (2014). Are the behaviors of transformational leaders impacting organizations?: A study of transformational leadership. *International Management Review, 10,* 5-9.

Bryman, A. (2012). *Social research methods.* New York, NY: Oxford University Press.

Buchner, A., Erdfelder, E., Faul, F., & Lang, A. G. (2009). Statistical power analyses using G*Power 3.1: Tests for correlation and regression analyses. *Behavior Research Methods, 41,* 1149-1160. doi:10.3758/BRM.41.4.1149

Buckley, O., Creese, S., Goldsmith, M., & Legg, P. A. (2015). Caught in the act of an insider attack: Detection and assessment of insider threat. *In Technologies for Homeland Security, IEEE International Symposium.* Retrieved from http://ieeexplore.ieee.org/

Chatterjee, S., Sarker, S., Valacich, J. S. (2015). The behavioral roots of information systems security: Exploring key factors related to unethical IT use. *Journal of Management Information Systems, 31,* 49-87. doi:10.1080/07421222.2014.100 1257

Chui, W. H., Sherry, M., & Thomas, P. (2010). International students: A vulnerable student population. *Higher Education, 60,* 33-46. doi:10.1007/s10734-009-9284-z

Clements, L. H., & Shawver, T. J. (2014). Are there gender differences when professional accountants evaluate moral intensity for earnings management? *Journal of Business Ethics,* 1-10. doi:10.1007/s10551-014-2293-6

Cohen, J. (1992). A power primer. *Psychological Bulletin, 112*(1), 155-159. doi:10.1037/0033-2909.112.1.155

Dalton, D., & Radtke, R. R. (2013). The Joint Effects of Machiavellianism and Ethical Environment on Whistle-Blowing. *Journal of Business Ethics, 117,* 153-172. doi:10.1007/s10551-012-1517-x

Danitz, S. B., & Orsillo, S. M. (2014). The mindful way through the semester: An investigation of the effectiveness of an acceptance-based behavioral therapy program on psychological wellness in first-year students. *Behavior Modification, 38,* 549-566. doi:10.1177/01145445513520218

Davis, B., Powell, S., & Read, B. (2014). Exploring employee misconduct in the workplace: Individual, organizational, and opportunity factors. *Journal of Academic and Business Ethics, 8.* Retrieved from http://www.aabri.com/

De Hoogh, A., den Hartog, D., & Kalshoven, K. (2013). Ethical leadership and follower helping and courtesy: Moral awareness and empathic concern as moderators. *Applied Psychology, 62,* 211-235. doi:10.1111/j.1464-0597.2011.00483.x

Dickerson, E. B., Festervand, T. A., & Vitell, S. J. (2000). Ethical problems, conflicts, and beliefs of small business professionals. *Journal of Business Ethics, 28,* 15-24. doi:10.1023/A:1006217129077

Doyle, S. P., Lount, R. B., Pettit, N. C., & To, C. (2016). Cheating to get ahead or to avoid falling behind? The effect of potential negative versus positive status change on unethical behavior. *Organizational Behavior and Human Decision Processes, 137,* 172-183. Retrieved from http://www.sciencedirect.com/science/

Fisher, J. A., & Monahan, T. (2015). Strategies for obtaining access to secretive or guarded organizations. *Journal of Contemporary Ethnography, 44,* 709-736. doi:10.1177/0891241614549834

Fryer, M. (2015). A role for ethics theory in speculative business ethics teaching. *Journal of Business Ethics, 1,* 1-12. doi:10.1007/s10551-015-2592-6

Gasper, J., Laufer, W. S., Warren, D. (2014). Is formal ethics training merely cosmetic? A study of ethics training and ethical organization culture. *Business Ethics Quarterly, 24,* 85-117. doi:10.5840/beq2014233

Gino, F. (2015). Understanding ordinary unethical behavior: Why people who value morality act immorally. *Behavioral Sciences, 3,* 107-111. doi:10.1016/j.cobeha.2015.03.001

Gino, F., Moore, C., Ruedy, N. E., & Schweitzer, M. E. (2014). The cheater's high: The unexpected affective benefits of unethical behavior. *Journal of Personality and Social Psychology, 105,* 531-548. doi:10.1037/a0034231

Gonzalez-Canton, C., Rohlfer, S., & Slocum, A. (2014). Teaching business ethics through strategically integrated mirco-insertions. *Journal of Business Ethics, 125,* 45-58. doi:10.1007/s10551.013.1905-x

Gove, S., & Janney, J. J. (2011). Reputation and corporate social responsibility aberrations, trends, and hypocrisy: Reactions to firm choices in the stock option backdating scandal. *Journal of Management Studies, 48,* 1562–1585. doi:10.1111/j.1467-6486.2010.00984.x

Harris, A. (2000). Is ethical attitudes among college students: A comparative study. *The Proceeding of ISECON* (Philadelphia, PA), 801-807. Retrieved from http://proc.isecon.org/2000/801/

Heckathorn, D. D. (2011). Comment: Snowball versus respondent-driven sampling. *Sociological Methodology, 41,* 355-366. doi:10.1111/j.1467-9531.2011.01244.x

Hersh, R. H., & Kohlberg, L. (1977). Moral development: A review of the theory. *Theory into Practice, 16,* 53-59. doi:10.1080/00405847709542675

Hrncir, T., Metts, S., & Smith, G. S. (2013). Small business fraud and the trusted employee. *Association of Certified Fraud Examiners, XX,* Retrieved from http://www.acfe.com/

Jackson, R. W., Wood, C. M., & Zboja, J. J. (2013). The dissolution of ethical decision making in organizations: A comprehensive review and model. *Journal of Business Ethics, 109,* 1-18. doi:10.1007/s10551-012-1459-3

Jeston, S., McDonald, S., & Pollock, W. (2014). A survey of inotrope and vaso-pressor line change practices in Australian and New Zealand neonatal intensive care units. *Journal of Neonatal Nursing, 20,* 69-76. doi:10.1016/j.jnn.2013.08.001

Lach, D. (2014). Challenges of interdisciplinary research: Reconciling qualitative and quantitative methods for understanding human landscape systems. *Environmental Management, 53,* 88-93. doi:10.1007/s00267-013-0115-8

Leggett, T., & Yates, J. (2016). Qualitative research: An introduction. *Radiologic Technology, 88,* 225-231.

Lehnert, K., Park, Y., & Singh, N. (2015). *Journal of Business Ethics, 129,* 195-219. doi:10.1007/s10551-014-2147-2

Luth, M. T., May, D. R., & Schwoerer, C. E. (2014). The influence of business ethics education on moral efficacy, moral meaningfulness, and moral courage: A quasi-experimental study. *Journal of Business Ethics, 124,* 67-80. doi:10.1007/s10551-013-1860.6

Mayer, D. M., Nurmohamed, S., Schminke, M., Shapiro, D. L., & Trevino, L. K. (2013). Encouraging employees to report unethical conduct internally: It takes a village. *Organizational Behavior and Human Decision Processes, 121,* 89-103. doi:10.1016/j.obhdp.2013.01.002

Pendse, S. G. (2012). Ethical hazards: A motive, means, and opportunity approach to curbing corporate unethical behavior. *Journal of Business Ethics, 107,* 265-279. doi:10.1007/s10551-011-1037-0

Peters, M. A., & Reveley, J. (2014). Retrofitting Drucker: Knowledge work under cognitive capitalism. *Journal of Culture and Organization, 20,* 135-151. doi:10.1080.14.759551.2012.692591

Pierce, L., & Snyder, J. A. (2015). Unethical demand and employee turnover. *Journal of Business Ethics, 131,* 853-869. doi:10.1007/s10551-013-2018-2

Pitesa, M., & Thau, S. (2013). Compliant sinners, obstinate saints: How power and self-focus determine the effectiveness of social influences in ethical decision making. *Academy of Management Journal, 56,* 635-658. doi:10.5465/amj.2011.0891

Raile, E. D. (2013). Building ethical capital: Perceptions of ethical climate in the public sector. *Public Administration Review, 73,* 253-262. doi:10.1111/j.1540-6210.2012.02649.x

Report to the nations. (2016, n.d.). Retrieved from http://www.acfe.com/

Schwartz, M. S. (2012). Developing and sustaining an ethical corporate culture: The core elements. *Business Horizons, 36*, 39-50. doi:10.1016/j. bushor.2012.09.002

Timofeyev, Y. (2014). Analysis of predictors of organizational losses due to occupational corruption. *International Business Review, 24*, 630-641. doi:10.1016/j. ibusrev.2014.11.007

Weber, J. (2014). Investigating and assessing the quality of employee ethics training programs among US-based global organizations. *Journal of Business Ethics, 127*, 1-16. doi:10.1007/s10551-014-2128-5

Wright, C. S. (2013). Developing ethical leaders: Is there inconsistency between theory and practice. *Journal of Human Values, 19*, 29-38. doi:10.1177/ 0971685812470329

Xinxin, L., & Yidong, T. (2013). How ethical leadership influence employees' innovative work behavior: A perspective of intrinsic motivation. *Journal of Business Ethics, 116*, 441-455. doi:10.1007/s10551-012-1455-7

Zuber, F. (2015). Spread of unethical behaviour in organizations: A dynamic social network perspective. *Journal of Business Ethics, 131*, 151-172. doi:10.1007/ s10551-014-2270-0

About the Author...

Dr. Karen J. Tillman resides in Maryland. Dr. Karen currently works for the Department of Homeland Security (DHS) and is a faculty member at the University of Maryland Eastern Shore. Dr. Karen received her Bachelor of Science degree in Psychology from the University of Maryland University College; a Master degree in Applied Information Technology from Towson University, including a Post Baccalaureate Certificate in Information and Security Assurance; and her Doctorate of Business Administration (DBA), emphasis in Information Systems Management, from Walden University. Dr. Karen holds a Project Management Professional Certification from PMI in 2009, and the ITILv3 certification in 2009.

Dr. Karen has over 14 years of experience as a Senior Principal Project Leader managing large, complex multi-use software and hardware development projects. As a Senior Principal Project Leader, Dr. Karen cultivated an environment of teamwork, team morale, integrity, promptness and good customer service.

Dr. Karen served in the U.S. Air Force and U.S. Army Reserves for a total of 12 years.

To reach Dr. Karen J. Tillman for information on business ethics, consulting, or guest speaking, please e-mail: drkjtillman@gmail.com

CHAPTER 7

Intrapreneurs:
The Lost Tribe

Dr. Susie Schild

Academia is reproached by companies and society for not producing critical thinkers with the ability to innovate and initiate entrepreneurial activities such as sustainability, cultural intelligence, leadership and ethical discourse (Persons, 2012; Tekarslan & Erden, 2014). Business leaders indicated a need for people to learn how to function as entrepreneurs and intrapreneurs focused on making businesses enterprises of good, not just better (Bradfield, 2009). Possibly these reproaches are reasons why Clay (2015) stated that though intrapreneurs are people who work to make a company better from the inside, as people they are a "lost tribe in corporate America" (Title). Finding the lost tribe of intrapreneurs prompted Fast Company and others to support contests such as *The League of Intrapreneurs: Building Better Business from the Inside Out,* to find employees with entrepreneurial skill sets. The act of seeking intrapreneurs with such an ambitious undertaking may suggest that intrapreneurs are not lost, as in extinct, but rather they remain hidden and not strictly of their own volition. History, the evolution of society, and Boudieu's (1998, 1986, 1977) publications on forms of capital may shed a light on the whereabouts of the lost tribe known as intrapreneurs. Refractive thinkers are keen observers, and can offer guidance toward finding intrapreneurs that create sustainable business success.

History of the word intrapreneur shows that during 1975–1980 the word *intrapreneur* made a debut (Dictionary.com, 2017).

Macrae (1982) credited Pinchot (1985) for the word intrapreneur in the article, *Intrapreneur Now,* based on research Pinchot published at the School for Entrepreneurs in Tarrytown, New York in 1978. The word intrapreneur used in an article published by Pinchot, described the practice of entrepreneurship within organizations. Popularity of the word intrapreneur came in a 1985 Newsweek article referring to the making of the team who developed the Macintosh computer, during an interview with Steve Jobs (Friday, 1985).

Locating one definition of intrapreneur proved challenging as many surfaced during this research; however, the simplistic tenets seem to be echoed in a quote from Elaine Beaubien, owner of Management Training Solutions and faculty for management and marketing for over 20 years at Edgewood College. Beaubin (n.d.) stated, "An intrepreneur is someone who displays the same characteristics as an Entrepreneur, but remains with an organization as an employee. They generate enterprise for the organization rather than create their own small business" (para. 2). As leaders seek to find intrapreneurs in their businesses, this research sought to find the same to make the definition a good fit.

Through a dozen web searches and 50 articles, two spellings emerged, intrapreneur and intrepreneur. Chosen for the purposes of this research is the spelling *intrapreneur.* Intrapreneur, also referred to in current literature as the corporate entrepreneur (Lavis, 2016). The word *intrapreneur* has roots from Pinchot's (1978) research, which used the phrase *intra-corporate entrepreneur.* Beyond the forming of the word, intrapreneur, since the publications of Pinchot (1978) and Macrae (1982), the *lost* situation of intrapreneurs seems little advanced as of the writing of this research.

In 1982, Macrae stated that the best-selling business books of the 1960s were the primary resources in academics a decade later, promoting the hierarchical structure, big business, and economy of scale as the way to achieve success. Macrae noted in the 1982 publication that small businesses or small workgroups were already outperforming big companies in almost every way. Further, Macrae sited case studies from Japanese businesses that instituted intrapreneurial endeavors and certain characteristics, attributing partial business success to not engaging in the teachings of business schools. Since the time of best-selling business books noted by Macrae in the 1960s, over half a century later, the writings of Bradfield (2009), Persons (2012), Tekarslan and Erden (2014) echoed similar problems, and reasons for lagging business success. Some of these reasons are a lack of teaching intrapreneurial skills and the popularization of big business. Refractive thinkers have these intrapraneurial skills, they see a problem differently, invite multiple perspectives toward a solution, and thus help companies create a more sustainable outcome.

A Problem

Salarzehi and Forouharfar's (2011) identified a general problem and proposed that to have flourishing and successful companies, knowing the general and specific barriers for companies is necessary. Considering Salarzehi and Forouharfar's proposal, barriers may be insightful to understanding businesses that fail. Federal Deposit Insurance Corporation data, focused on the financial industry, documented the liquidation, merger, or government nationalization of 553 U.S. financial institutions since October 1, 2000 through May 26, 2017 (2017). These business failures are important considering the reliance on financial institutions by individuals day-to-day worldwide, and are the institutions that move money for commerce. Failure of such institutions prove to be disruptive to society as seen during *The Great Recession* (2007-2009). Regarding the viability of institutions in general, Salarzehi and Forouharfar suggested that products in the marketplace continually derive less value from labor or capital goods and more value from the "quality of thought and innovation imparted to the products" (2011, p. 491). Presumably, more quality intrapreneurial thought and innovation toward superior consumer products may assist in the sustainability of corporations and institutions. Quality of thought and innovation may be the fodder for corporate success in a competitive market place. Lavis (2016) indicated, intrapreneurship is key to the competitive marketplace and may be what organizations need as a strategy for sustainability and prevention of economic disruptions as seen in *The Great Recession.*

Automation, business, and product cycles continue to quicken pace to the marketplace, and denotes rapid change. With rapid change, workers need new skills to remain relevant and competitive (Lavis 2016, Schild, 2013). Employees have varying aspirations to assist their company and their company should have an interest in fostering the discovery and development of employees' ambitions (Lavis, 2016). Help from companies in the form of mentorship to guide employees toward relevancy and remaining competitive was a sentiment expressed by knowledge workers (Schild, 2013). Some of these workers are likely up and coming intrapreneurs. Govindarajan and Desai (2013) stated that out of 5,000 employees, at least 250 are innovators and at least 25 of those are intrapreneurs. These intrapreneurs want to make a sustainable contribution, which is something more than a paycheck (Santos & Williams, 2013). Santos and Williams (2013) further stated companies should exercise abundant opportunities for highly skilled employees or these people will leave for the desired opportunities, possibly with a competitor. Alternatively, they may become entrepreneurs in their own business, becoming a competitor or vendor. Either way, Chamorro-Premuzic (2012) stated, companies lose good people, including intrapreneurs, because leaders do not promote out of the box refractive thinking, largely because of the fear of losing the employee. Chamorro-Premuzic (2012) reported that entrepreneurs foster business ideas while working for companies, and with no process to leverage their ideas, they left. These ideas become start-ups that total over $3 trillion in U.S. gross domestic product (Chamorro-Premuzic, 2012). Business leaders, make no mistake interpreting the prior sentence, employees say you are not listening. These former intrapreneurs also stated their bosses were untenable, giving them one more reason to leave their companies and inadvertently stimulate entrepreneurship elsewhere (Chamorro-Premuzic, 2012). However, poor leadership causes more entrepreneurial failure than success. As such a specific problem emerges that companies lose intrapreneurs from their choices shaping capital forms and thus through their own volition. This problem is important to understand because the problem is led and may be solved from the same people inside organizations, leaders. Leaders in organizations pave the way for social constructs including the inclusiveness of ideas from all levels of employee.

Intrapreneurial Traits and Characteristics

The intrapreneurial examples in the upcoming section, demonstrate several intrapreneurial traits and characteristics. Beaubin (n.d.) cited the following traits of intrapreneurs, they: are risk takers, trust themselves, learn from mistakes, see opportunities, display passion, and provide a unique experience for their customers. Additionally, a study by Farrukh, Ying, and Shaheen (2016) suggested that extroversion, openness to experience, and emotional stability as the main behavioral traits for intrapreneurs. Norms toward intrapreneurs are valuable to know and cultivate in ourselves and others; however, the traits and characteristics most commonly found need not be the only artifacts that denote an intrapreneur.

Yershon (n.d.), from Ogilvy Labs, stated intrapreneurs get out of their comfort zone and they hunt (Institute of Promotional

Marketing Ltd). Yershon promoted different ways of achieving goals and thus different ways of thinking critical to intrapreneurship. Therefore, commonly held beliefs may not always be the way to intrapreneurialism. In the search for intrapreneurs, one might say, not everyone possesses the common traits or characteristics of intrapreneurs and as such intrapreneurs may not walk like a common duck, and should not be fixed to walk like one either. Yershon gave the example of an employee that goes to many kinds of shows and learns a broad range of information. The employee enjoys trade shows across industries, and has a dyslexic condition, which may be what enables the production of work that the company finds valuable. Yershon described this employee as unconventional. To change employees to fit into company norms, would not produce intrapreneurial value. Yershon stated, the employee is a hunter and helps the company break ties with their traditional preconceptions.

Intrapreneur Experiences

Reports of intrapreneurial experiences are broad and range from engagement in projects that bring new products and revenue to ideas that bring incremental change assisting in financial savings for organizations. Introduced in the following paragraphs are a range of intrapreneurial experiences. Each experience presented below is related to research to help understand the experience expressed through forms of capital and how that experience scaffolds toward an understanding of volition.

Intrapreneurs can achieve sustainable success for companies and sometimes stay long after the launch of a new venture. The Thunderbird School of Global Management (Thunderbird), ranked 4th in the world, per Quacquarelli Symonds (2017), for their Online MBA, prospered by promoting the intrapreneur spirit. Thunderbird supported an intrapreneurial venture with Mansour Javidan

Ph.D., Distinguished Garvin Professor. That venture became the Najafi Global Mindset Institute (personal communication with Dr. Javidan, August 1, 2017). The Najafi Global Mindset Institute studies the qualities that make international managers successful through defining, measuring, and developing global mindset (Pivotal Group, n.d.). Dr. Javidan explained that the Institute engages the experiences of world class businesses and business schools and uses the data to help business and academic ventures succeed (personal communication August 1, 2017).

Dr. Javidan did not know how to accomplish the task or what the idea would look like in the end, but his employer afforded him the resources to take a risk and build something new (personal communication with Dr. Javidan, August 1, 2017). Using his intrapreneurial skills, Dr. Javidan built an idea, and launched the institute in 2011. As of the writing of this article, Dr. Javidan still teaches and consults all over the world for Thunderbird as the Director of the Najafi Global Mindset Institute. Not always the case, yet in this example, the institution gave the intrapreneur the requisite resources to stay and continue to foster the business venture.

According to Bourdieu's (1986) forms of capital, Dr. Javidan seemingly had enough relative cultural capital in all its forms, embodied, objectified, and institutionalized, to mobilize his skills and lead a successful intrapreneurial venture. Specifically, Dr. Javidan's PhD credentials gave him what Bourdieu referred to as the requisite institutionalized cultural capital to succeed. Academic dialect mastered as part of the credentialing process provided requisite embodied cultural capital. This intrapreneur had enough collective identity to fit in and succeed. By the companies own volition, the company made a conscious effort to help Dr. Javidan and the Najafi Global Mindset Institute succeed.

Sometimes internally sponsored intrapreneurial ventures do not workout (Conversations Staff, 2012). The intrapreneurial product, *new Coke,* lacked popularity with consumers. Coke's then Chief Executive Officer, Mr. Goizueta, stated that *new Coke* was a prime example of taking intelligent risks. Goizueta further stated, engaging in intelligent risk indicated that the company would do what was necessary to increase value for the company's owners.

Important to notice is why the *new* Coke venture launched in the first place and the alignment, being owner value. Value for a select group in an organization is not always in alignment with the value intrapreneurs seek to create. Santos and Williams (2013) suggested social intrapreneurs seek to innovate social impact using company resources, and profit not the primary concern or outcome. As Millennials continue to become a driving force in the workplace, McNally (2016) suggested that Millennials want to change outdated systems, independently work outside the traditional system, and do good, not just make good profits. A focus on owner value such as in the Coke example, may be at odds with Millennial values engaged in social intrapreneurship. Owner value seems to diverge from a focus Bradfield (2009) promoted, where intrapreneurs focus on making businesses enterprises of good, not just better. In this example, the customer was not the focus of value and the conscious volition on the part of leadership toward a single goal of owner profit did not turn out for the betterment of the organization. The lesson for leaders is to understand consciously, the goals and effort that the company puts forth and for whom the effort will produce value. The value created for many (the customers) outweighs the needs of the few (the owners).

Another example from Lockheed Martin is the Skunk Works project (Kneece, 2014). Here an idea produced innovative and successful aircraft models. The intrapreneur had resources, autonomy, and he was also the founder of the company. People at the top may have leverage to pitch their ideas and thus an advantage toward intrapreneurship. The Lockheed example demonstrates that the intrapreneur possessed requisite cultural capital, especially institutionalized cultural capital with his position in the company. Bourdieu (1986) pointed out that some forms of cultural capital have higher value than others, and can hinder or assist one's social mobility, including the mobility of ideas from employees with devalued cultural capital. Understanding varied value in capital, may further support Kneece (2014) who noted companies block innovation by job function. Hierarchical structure and job function can be just as much a disadvantage to intrapreneurship. The Skunk Works example may shed light on why lower level and budding intrapreneurs' ideas are left waiting out in the cold. The takeaway for leaders is that the employees function does not set a limit for their ideas and contributions across the organization. Devalued capital in the form of a job title is the visible artifact of the company's conscious volition toward hierarchy.

Ideas come from all levels of employee and if the company listens they gain the knowledge of their human capital. All intrapreneurial ideas are not game changers for a company; some are incremental, sustaining and come from employees outside of what the company might expect. A guard suggested changing from film to digital pictures at the Massachusetts Department of Corrections (Kneece, 2014). In the first year of implementation across 16 facilities, the department saved $56,000 in film alone. As explained by Bourdieu (1986) institutionalized cultural capital, meaning the organizational culture and social interplay, allowed the intrapreneur to maneuver the social field and thus play a part in an intrapreneurial experience. Important to understand is that the social field is constructed by the players, being the employees and leaders of the company. Leaders pave the way for social constructs having the required symbolic capital of the hierarchical structure, in other words their leader title. This example enlightens companies to the reality that intrapreneurial thinking can come from any employee and the culture of the company in its various forms allows or disallows the ideas that enable a company to harness intrapreneurship to their benefit.

A personal conversation with K. Otis on September 26, 2017 revealed attempts at intrapreneurship. Holding several roles throughout this career, including management positions, K. Otis found organizational cultures inhospitable. In corporate America, observations included that one must fit in with the right people for the opportunity to pitch ideas and thought of as a serious contributor. Bourdieu (1986) stated that some forms of cultural capital have higher value than others which may help explain the interviewee's sentiments. K. Otis, a self-described artist, remains accomplished in this craft and successful in these corporate roles (personal communication, September 26, 2017). Prepared with the requisite command of skills, drive, ethics, and savvy of an intrapreneur, as a Black American, *fitting in* was to difficult to overcome. K. Otis left corporate life and became an entrepreneur, owning a business, and seeking opportunities with a better fit (September 26, 2017). K. Otis stated that other Black Americans relay a similar story regarding the barrier of color, which invites the perspective of layered constructs of habitus at play in forms of capital.

The broad ideology of cultural capital includes a sense of collective identity (Bourdieu, 1986), which K. Otis did not experience. Social capital, not independent of other forms of capital, interplays across forms of capital and reveals itself through the lack of group membership experience (Bourdieu, 1986). This experience may show what Bourdieu (1986) meant by some forms of capital have higher value than others, and can hinder or assist one's social mobility. Had the experience included group membership, the chances of collective identity may increase. By the accounts of the above interview not *fitting in,* a lack of cultural and social capital, diminished the possibilities of intrapreneurship. Walker (2009) suggested that successful black entrepreneurs are limited as were pre-civil war blacks to remove race-based institutional and societal constraints that diminish gains in forms of capital and business success. Leaders of business constructing the current forms of capital by which their organizations succeed, or fail, do so of their own volition.

These examples show forms of capital and habitus underpin the very nature of intrapreneurial expressions and the journey of a business venture. Intrapreneurship is not strictly about the characteristics that make up an intrapreneur. Even if, as Bradfield (2009), Persons (2012), and Tekarslan and Erden (2014) suggested, that business schools teach intrapreneurial skills and dispel big business as the behemoth of success, paradigms, and the habitus of organizations must change.

Intrapreneurship Lost

Limited by our situational and traditional preconceptions, the evolution of paradoxes and paradigms in society aid in hiding the scope of change until the change advances to a new norm, for which only then is recognized. As a social construct, Bourdieu (1977) described the evolution of the norm as habitus, or regular practices and in no way an outcome of compliance to rules. Thus, many reasons may play into why intrapreneurship may be considered lost. Change in the physical world that possibly contributed to the lost intrapreneur, was the advent of the cotton gin in 1793, signaling the arrival of automation on the farm (Douglas, 1982). Independent farmers, not beholden to another for livelihood, began to disappear. Concentrations of capital and changes to laws fueled big business and dependent wage earners emerged.

This example above, provided by Douglas (1982), serves as a reference point of change in economic, social, cultural, and symbolic capital. People traded, subjugated, or lost at least some of their free thinking and freewill as they exchanged their time and skill that benefited another for a paycheck. The capital-intensive technologies demanded large numbers of workers and challenged farming life's social and economic capital (Bomboy, 2017; Douglas, 1982). The paradigm of agrarian culture began to split and shift toward a paradox between the agrarian and the machine age. Imaginably, attached meaning and thus symbolic capital shifted for both farm and machine work. Forming these new habits of work, economic dependencies, and social symbolic meaning, created new habits by subjugating oneself to that of the larger organizational operation. Creating habits through action is a social construct, and describes the evolution of the norm as habitus, or regular practices (Bourdieu,1977). These afore mentioned social changes help clarify that forms of capital are within the power of people in organizations to change, just as people made a change from a self-sustaining to a dependent economic society.

When people stop working for themselves and their ideas become subservient to that of the business for which they work, the propensity for tensions to arise as the work the employee performs departs further from their own values and ideas increases. Research conducted in Iran with an organization that has a mission to promote entrepreneurship indicated that tensions between the values of intrapreneurs and their organization, was the principal barrier to intrapreneurship (Salarzehi & Forouharfar, 2011). Values may be key, as Hult News (2015) stated, an "employee with the right outlook can help an organization derive greater value" (para. 7), and a dynamic and collaborative workplace is beneficial to intrapreneurship. Values and expectations in compliant and hierarchical environments may be a barrier to intrapreneurship. Alignment of values between the company and intrapreneurs may increase the chances for intrapreneurs to add value, while misalignment may leave intrapreneurs unable to contribute or lost.

Demographic characteristics influence intrapreneurs' personal values (Camillo et al., 2012). These characteristics are firm size, product type, creative background, business background, educational level, age, personal values, and innovation performance. Such characteristics identified by Camillo et al., (2012) align with entrepreneurial resources and capabilities recognized as factors of intrapreneurship, such as the ability to detect business opportunities, entrepreneurial competences, and previous entrepreneurial experience (Urbano, Alvarez, & Turró, 2013). The effect of these entrepreneurial resources and capabilities influence intrapreneurial behavior. Businesses wanting intrapreneurship as a cultural and individual worker characteristic must engage strategically in the acquisition of intrapreneurship as a volitionary act.

Corporate entrepreneurs' cognitive ability to discover, create, and successfully exploit opportunities (Gaglio, 2004) and their learning models (Bingham et al., 2007; Corbett, 2005), are resources and capabilities that mediate intrapreneurial behavior and contribute to the management of personal knowledge. Stankosky (2005) suggested that employee resources and capabilities are commodities of the knowledge worker, or intrapreneur, mediated by inherent social capital and thus mobilized (Dang & McKelvey, 2016). Social capital, one of the four forms of capital theorized by Bourdieu (1986), illuminates the problem that companies lose intrapreneurs through their own volition. Companies are not entities of thought, they are the constructs of human thought process, and as such intrapreneurs are lost only to the constructs of habitus and capital forms. Bourdieu explained that the network of capital is not given naturally, meaning just because we are human, nor is it socially given. Constituted by action, capital is the product of investment in establishing and reproducing social relationship usable across time and transforms workplaces into lasting subjectively felt obligations or guaranteed institutional rights.

Considering the historic implications of social capital, change to some business paradigms are taking place that may be favorable to intrapreneurs. The flattening of hierarchical titles such as director and manager to a single title of *associate* for all at Gore

Industries, may level the psychological playing field and promote more equality toward the ideas each employee brings to the workplace. Open work environments at Zappos may prove to mitigate distance from upper management and again promote idea equality and thus intrapreneurship. Possibly the mindset of the Millennials and social entrepreneurship will assist in moderating hierarchical social capital referred to by Dang and McKelvey (2016), and give rise to opportunities for rank and file intrapreneurial participation, and thus find lost intrapreneurs. McNally (2016) suggested Millennials have a tribe mentality, which may give them a louder voice in the way work is done. Limited by current situational perceptions, society may hear only the static of intrapreneurs' voices and not yet see the lost tribe reemerging.

Conclusion

A reemergence of intrapreneurs comes four centuries after automation on farms in the 1700s that began the journey of intrapreneurs into the twenty-first century (Douglas, 1982). The phenomenon of lost intrapreneurialism has not gone unnoticed as demonstrated in publications from Macrae (1982) and Pinchot (1978). Social paradigms of tradition, paradoxes of growth, and forms of capital, such as symbolism in hierarchical business structure, played a part in the evolutionary situation of intrapreneurs. The value of capital forms persists through the outcomes of human action such as the closure of large and small businesses, including fiduciary companies, and constitutes a societal paradigm. Intrapreneurial interventions can inculcate sustainability through innovation in organizations.

The reemergence of the intrapreneur invokes a flattening of the hierarchy, pushing authority down, and having a culture that authentically values what everybody in the company brings to work is as important as what a C-level employee brings (Kingl,

2017). Values alignment may play a key role in assisting companies and intrapreneurs to have a more productive relationship (Hult News, 2015). Thus, the artifacts of a company must align with tenets of intrapreneurship and reasonably to the values of the intrapreneur.

Demographic characteristics influence intrapreneurs' personal values, and value alignment includes demographic characteristics that influence intrapreneurs' personal values (Camillo et al., 2012). Understanding the value of forms of capital as psychological constructs, allows an understanding that capital is within the power of people to change. Establishing and reproducing social relationship usable across time, transforms workplaces into sustainable subjective obligations (Bourdieu, 1986). This research suggests that intrapreneurs are lost to symbolic, social, economic, and the physical embodiment of cultural capital, habitus. Forms of capital and habitus are human constructs and leaders who, hear the voices of generations, allow equality of ideas regardless of ranks, titles, education, or fortune, and make a strategic choice toward finding intrapreneurs. Refractive thinkers embody the intrapreneurial spirit and are keen observers, that can offer guidance toward finding the intrapreneur tribe in an organization and create sustainable success.

THOUGHTS FROM THE ACADEMIC ENTREPRENEUR

The problem to be solved:

- Companies lose intrapreneurs through their own volition.

The goals:

- Raise awareness of intrapreneurs, and the benefits they bring to the success of companies.
- Create a culture of intrapreneurship.
- Question paradigms.

The questions to ask:

- How can intrapreneurs forge themselves in organizations?
- Can organizations cultivate intrapreneurs in all levels of employee?
- Is a business staying in their comfort zone or are they hunting to make businesses enterprises of good?
- Is the business listening to the voice of a tribe mentality in Millennials?

Today's Business Application:

- Effective leaders understand the tension employees face in acting as intrapreneurs.
- Inclusion of intrapreneurial efforts through change to paradigms and paradoxes created through forms of capital.
- Knowing the barriers to intrapreneurship, could help leaders in companies to face these barriers and moderate the effect towards sustainability and prosperity.
- Foster intrapreneurship for the sustainability of the company. A trend of high turnover and low tenure often bemoaned by HR and leaders alike is manageable by companies if they choose.

- Delegate and thus empower aspiring intrapreneurs to grow and provide value.

- Leaders need ideas to implement and continue to make companies successful. Listen to the ideas of employees regardless of title, education, or academic degree who are passionate enough about their ideas that they want to speak. They may also want the opportunity to take responsibility and see their idea come alive.

REFERENCES

Bingham, C., Eisenhardt, K., & Furr, N. (2007). What makes a process a capability?: Heuristics, strategy and effective capture of opportunities. *Strategic Entrepreneurship Journal, 1*, 27-47. doi:10.1002/sej.1

Bomboy, S. (2017, March 14). The cotton gin: A game-changing social and economic invention [Web log post]. Retrieved from https://constitutioncenter.org/blog/the-cotton-gin-a-game-changing-social-and-economic-invention

Bourdieu, P. (1977). *Outline of a theory of practice.* Cambridge, MA: Cambridge University Press.

Bourdieu, P. (1986). The forms of capital. In J. Richardson (Ed.) *Handbook of Theory and Research for the Sociology of Education* (pp. 241-258). New York, NY: Greenwood.

Bourdieu, P. (1998). *Practical reason: On the theory of action.* Stanford, CA: Stanford University Press.

Bradfield S. L. (2009). The value of sustainability education. *Journal of Management Education, 33,* 372-375. doi:10.1177/1052562908327638

Beaubin, E. (n.d.). Intrepreneurs: Use them or lose them. *Capturing the Essence of Excellence* [Web log post]. Retrieved from https://sites.google.com/site/elainebeaubien/why-train/articles/intrepreneurship

Camillo, C., Fernández-Alles, M., Ruiz-Navarro, J., & Ginel, E. S. (2012). The intrapreneur and innovation in creative firms, *International Small Business Journal 30,* 513-535. doi:10.1177/0266242610385396

Clay, A. (2015, November 15). The rise of the intrapreneurs: Discovering a lost tribe in corporate America: The people trying to make it better from the inside, *Fast Company.* Retrieved from https://www.fastcompany.com/2680655/the-rise-of-the-intrapreneurs

Chamorro-Premuzic, T. (2012, September 10). How bad leadership spurs entrepreneurship, *Harvard Business Review.* Retrieved from https://hbr.org/2012/09/how-bad-leadership-spurs-entrepreneurship

Conversations Staff. (2012, November 14). The real story of new Coke. *The Coca-Cola Company.* Retrieved from http://www.coca-colacompany.com/stories/coke-lore-new-coke

Corbett, A. (2005). Experiential learning within the process of opportunity identification and exploitation. *Entrepreneurship Theory and Practice, 4,* 473-491. doi:10.1111/j.1540-6520.2005.00094.x

Dang, R. J., & McKelvey, M. (2016). Knowledge management processes and the formation of entrepreneurial opportunities. *Journal of Innovation Economics & Management, 1*(19), 31-59. doi:10.3917/jie.019.0031

Douglas, J. D. (1982, November 1). A rebirth of economic freedom: The de-bureaucratization of American business. *The Foundation for Economic Education.* Retrieved from https://fee.org/articles/a-rebirth-of-economic-freedom-the-de-bureaucratization-of-american-business/

Farrukh, M., Ying, C. W., & Mansori, S. (2016). Intrapreneurial behavior: An empirical investigation of personality traits. *Management & Marketing, 11*, 597-609. doi:10.1515/mmcks-20160018

FDIC (2017, September 7). *Failed bank list.* Retrieved from https://www.fdic.gov/bank/individual/failed/banklist.html

Friday, C. (1985, September 25). Showdown in Silicon Valley. *Newsweek.* Retrieved from http://www.newsweek.com/showdown-silicon-valley-207014

Gaglio, C. (2004). The role of mental simulations and counterfactual thinking in the opportunity identification process, *Entrepreneurship Theory and Practice, 28,* 533-552. doi:10.1111/j.1540-6520.2004.00063.x

Govindarajan, V., & Desai, J. (2013, September 20). Recognize intrapreneurs before they leave, *Harvard Business Review.* Retrieved from https://hbr.org/2013/09/recognize_intrapreneurs

Hult News. (2015). Intrapreneurs: Why big businesses value the entrepreneurial mindset [Web log post]. Retrieved from http://www.hult.edu/news/intrapreneurs-big-businesses-value-entrepreneurial-mindset/

Institute of Promotional Marketing Ltd. (n.d.). *How to be an intrapreneur.* Retrieved from https://www.theipm.org.uk/insights/the-union-of-marketing-and-technology-2014/how-to-be-an-intrepreneur.aspx

Kingl, A. (2015, January 1). The rise of the Intrapreneur: Forward-thinking companies are stealing a march on their competitors, *London Business School* [Web log post]. Retrieved from https://www.london.edu/faculty-and-research/lbsr/the-rise-of-the-intrapreneur#.WcPpy8iGPIU

Kneece, K. (2014, September 17). 10 inspiring examples of successful intrapreneurship. *Innovation Insights* [Web log post]. Retrieved from http://insights.wired.com/profiles/blogs/10-inspiring-examples-of-successful-intrapreneurship#axzz-4tALHNSjJ

Lavis, I. (2016, December 16). Rise of the intrapreneur: Why corporate entrepreneurship is key to competitiveness, *Business Review Europe* [Web log post]. Retrieved from http://www.businessrevieweurope.eu/leadership/1189/Rise-of-the-intrapreneur:-why-corporate-entrepreneurship-is-key-to-competitiveness

McNally, B. W. (2016, October 3). The future of work and employee engagement through the lens of Millennials. *Sustainable Brands.* Retrieved from http://www.sustainablebrands.com/news_and_views/organizational_change/brynn_mcnally/future_work_employee_engagement_through_lens_mill

Macrae, N. (1928, April 17). Intrapreneurial now. *The Economist.* Retrieved from https://www.intrapreneur.com/MainPages/History/Economist.html

Persons, O. (2012). Incorporating corporate social responsibility and sustainability into business course: A shared experience. *Journal of Education for Business,* *87,* 63-72. doi:10.1080/08832323.2011.562933

Pinchot, G. (1985). *Intrapreneuring: Why you don't have to leave the corporation to become an entrepreneur,* New York, NY: Harper & Row.

Pivotal Group (n.d.). *Najafi Global Mindset Institute launches at Thunderbird.* Retrieved from http://pivotalgroup.com/pr_9-13-11.htm

Quacquarelli Symonds Limited. (2017). *QS Distance Online MBA Rankings 2017.* Retrieved from https://www.topmba.com/mba-rankings/online-mba-rankings/2017#sorting=rank+custom=856098+order=+search=

Salarzehi, H., & Forouharfar, A. (2011). Understanding barriers to intrapreneurship in work and social affairs governmental organization (A case study in Iran). *Interdisciplinary Journal of Contemporary Research in Business, 2,* 490-503. Retrieved from http://www.ijcrb.com/

Santos, F., & Williams, J. (2013, November 7). *The rise of the social intrapreneur* [Web log post]. Retrieved from https://knowledge.insead.edu/responsibility/the-rise-of-the-social-intrapreneur-2961

Schild, S. (2013). *Personal knowledge management for employee commoditization* (Doctoral dissertation). Retrieved from ProQuest Dissertations & Theses Global database. (UMI No. 3574622)

Stankosky, M. (2005). Advances in knowledge management: University research toward an academic discipline. In M. Stankosky (Ed.), *Creating the discipline of knowledge management: The latest in university research* (pp. 1-14). Burlington, MA: Elsevier Butterworth-Heinemann.

Tekarslan, E., & Erden, N. S. (2014). A review of business education around the globe: Future transitions. *Journal of Multidisciplinary Research, 6*(2), 49-64. Retrieved from http://www.jmrpublication.org/Default.aspx

Urbano, D., Alvarez, C., & Turró, A. (2013). Organizational resources and intrapreneurial activities: An international study. *Management Decision, 51,* 854-870. doi:10.1108/00251741311326617

Walker, J. E. K. (2009). *The history of black business in America: Capitalism race, entrepreneurship Volume I.* Chapel Hill, NC: The University of North Carolina Press.

About the Author ...

Currently a resident of Arizona, Dr. Susie A. Schild holds several accredited degrees; a Bachelor of Arts (BA) from California State University Long Beach; a Master of Management (MM) from University of Phoenix; and a Doctorate of Education (Ed.D / ET) in Educational Leadership with a specialization in Educational Technology from the University of Phoenix School of Advanced Studies. She holds two Knowledge Management Certifications from Knowledge Management Professional Society, and is Lean Six Sigma green belt certified.

Dr. Schild has enjoyed time working with students in UC Berkley's popular MOOC course, *The Science of Happiness,* and currently, serves as Director of Learning Design for ADP.

To reach Dr. Susie Schild for information on consulting or doctoral coaching, please e-mail: susanschild00@gmail.com

CHAPTER 8

The Importance of Work/Life Balance as an Entrepreneur

Dr. Matt Motil

Work / life balance is a key element to success, particularly for the entrepreneur and business owner. Despite the subtle differences, the importance of passion as part of the motivation for success for the entrepreneur and the business owner is the foundation for success. In the academic community, researchers spend their entire careers on the *how* to help employers and employees balance work life and home life (Bria, Spânu, Băban, & Dumitraşcu, 2014; Maslach & Jackson, 1981; Maslach, Schaufeli, & Leiter, 2001; Pinto, Dawood, & Pinto, 2014)1981; Maslach, Schaufeli, & Leiter, 2001; Pinto, Dawood, & Pinto, 2014, only since 2015 has this focus on work life balance become part of the discussion for the entrepreneur. The Motil (2015) study focused specifically on burnout in construction management regarding project factors that might accelerate the burnout phenomenon among construction professionals. Only after leaving the employment space and starting a personal entrepreneurial journey as a business owner without a safety net did I realize the challenges regarding work / life balance as an entrepreneur and how different the burnout phenomenon exists predominantly for employees and seems to vanish for entrepreneurs. The purpose of this writing is to integrate emerging research about burnout and stress as an integral part of the entrepreneurial experience using the refractive thinking approach to examine why.

Freudenberger (1974) coined the term *burnout* in the 1970s in psychological research. Maslach and Jackson (1981) expanded this research in the early 1980s developing a multidimensional model of burnout. In the multidimensional model, the measurement of experienced burnout consisted of three components that act as legs of a stool with the phenomenon of burnout at the base, to include (a) emotional exhaustion, (b) cynicism, and (c) reduced personal efficacy (Maslach et al., 2001). Further, the Maslach Burnout Inventory–General Survey (MBI-GS) offered a modified version of the original assessment tool to focus on all professions, not just the human-services industry (Schaufeli, Leiter, Maslach, & Jackson, 1996). Further research placed the concept of burnout as a foundation using the conservation of resources theory as an individual strives to protect, collect, and construct that which they value (Alarcon, 2011). The concept works when an employee perceives a loss either through work or home life. The employee experiences a perceived tradeoff or loss, when an employer requires them to spend time at an activity or task when mentally they would rather invest their time elsewhere (Alarcon, 2011).

With the foundation of research of burnout dating back to the mid-1970s (Freudenberger, 1974), standing defiantly in the face of over 40 years of research and crying foul is a bold gesture. Reflecting on personal experience as an employee in the demanding industry of construction management, I experienced the effects of burnout firsthand. In reading study after study regarding burnout in the construction industry, the participants in these studies had very similar symptoms and experiences as my own (Lingard, Francis, & Turner, 2012; Lorente, Salanova, Martínez, & Vera, 2014; Mostert, 2011; Mostert, Peeters, & Rost, 2011; Shen, Tuuli, Xia, Koh, & Rowlinson, 2014; Turner & Lingard, 2014; Xie, Wu, Luo, & Hu, 2010; Zhang, Lee, Choi, & An, 2013).

Of additional interest, was that once I no longer worked in the industry I did not enjoy nor for someone else, the burnout phenomenon quickly vanished, despite working more hours per day and more days per week. Refractive thinking begs the question to dig deeper to examine why.

As an entrepreneur, one quickly realizes the only way to be successful is to be living, breathing, and working in one's passion daily. The importance of Maslow's (1954) Hierarchy of Needs shapes this conversation, acknowledging the personal need for self-satisfaction and personal growth and actualization. Once an entrepreneur achieves the ability to monetize their passion, they are no longer *working* (Motil, 2017). When what one spends their time doing is no longer perceived as work, no need exists to recover, escape, or balance (Charfen, 2015). Consequently, the irony of work life balance also disappears as one removes the work element from the equation. The three pillars of the burnout syndrome become unstable (Maslach, 1981).

Defining the Middle-Class Trap

For many Americans growing up in the 1980s and 1990s, two options existed for the high school graduate. One enrolled in college or entered the trades (Motil, 2017). One might consider joining a union to learn a skill or one went to college to focus on a more technical and credentialed path. For many graduates, with the aptitude to go to college, high school guidance counselors moved these eager students through the front doors of the college system across the country. The cultural expectation of becoming a self-sufficient member of society required one to (a) get good grades, (b) get a good job after graduation, (c) get married, (d) have kids, and subsequently (e) get themselves into debt (Motil, 2017). The cycle included the traditional path of paying off student loans that come due 6 months after graduation, perhaps taking on a home loan in the form of mortgages, car payments, and credit card bills, having children with their debt, and getting caught in this seemingly circuitous path of debt and leverage, a path difficult to escape. The

American Dream seemed a daunting challenging regarding managing expectations and harsh realities as one attempted to balance work and home (Charfen, 2015; Motil, 2017).

The reality is that many people remain confined within the limits of poverty, yet despite living in a poverty or project-type situation, the concept of debt is different. In many cases, a person may be (a) a victim of their location and their circumstances, (b) their upbringing, and (c) resultant mindset (Motil, 2017). The odd irony here is the lack of debt. Those in poverty do not have debt in the traditional sense of leveraged ownership. They owe no one. By contrast, as one moves into the middle and upper class, a different type of situation emerges, including for many crushing debt, justified by the ideas of success. The emerging reality is that leveraging debt as a precursor to success is a challenging way to define the American Dream, further exacerbating the idea of work life balance. One remains caught in a perpetual loop of the need to make more money to manage the leveraged debt, trading time for dollars, seemingly moving further and further away from balance, according to Maslow's (1954) needs. The rungs of the ladder in Maslow's hierarchy become more elusive, often out of reach for many (Abbe, Harvey, Ikuma, & Aghazadeh, 2011; An, Zhang, & Lee, 2013). As the employee attempts to fulfill the culturally accepted norms of what success looks like in the American Dream through leveraging debt, the snare of the trap tightens (Motil, 2017). Most employees can lead perfectly happy lives attempting to balance work life and home life (Bowen, Edwards, & Lingard, 2012, 2013; Bowen, Edwards, Lingard, & Cattell, 2013, 2014). For some, the internal ambition and drive pushes the employee for more. Alex Chafen (2015) described this drive and ambition that cannot be turned off as the Entrepreneurial Personality Type (EPT). Remaining satisfied in the trap, once identified, becomes extremely difficult for the ambitious employee (Motil, 2017). Ultimately, I chose to pursue my own path when I found myself in this situation.

Entrepreneurship

With a doctorate in business, a reasonable expectation of success seemed plausible for starting a company (Motil, 2017). Nothing could have been further from the truth when beginning my journey as an entrepreneur. Entering the business world as a sole proprietor is often the first step along this path (Motil, 2017). Challenges are vastly different with a small business with an employee of one, as opposed to building an organization with hiring employees, building a team, growing a team, and conducting personal development for the team, as one becomes truly responsible for the future of others beyond one's inner circle (Motil, 2017).

Mastering middle and upper management skills such as leadership, management, conflict management, and negotiation skills are roles that business skills prepare graduates to face (Motil, 2017). With training as an engineer with a years of experience working in industry, the transition appeared an easy path to take, particularly with additional academic credentials with a business degree. Academia included instruction in human resources (HR), and organizational development (OD), effective leadership and management theories, conflict management, and team development, which helps a current, established company go from good to better or better to great (Collins, 2001). Despite academic credentials of more than 24+ years of school to include higher education and personal experience of 20 years, I knew nothing about starting a company from scratch or building one once I did. Herein lies the challenge for those with higher education. Despite earning a doctorate degree with decades of credentialed education, significant holes existed within a graduate's knowledge that does not prepare many for having anything other than a job (Charfen, 2015). The cultural expectation of education includes the focus of creating employees, not business owners; moving to a new job instead of transitioning into the owner or creator of jobs (Motil, 2017).

Ultimately, while approximately 30 million companies exist in the United States, only about 22% of those have even one employee. (Small Business Administration [SBA], 2012) The clear majority of business owners become self-employed by definition, missing the mark of the purpose and passion of the entrepreneurial spirit entirely. The goal is to learn to balance life while building and leveraging other people's times, supporting the nature and concept of being an entrepreneur (Kiyosaki & Lechter, 1997). These concepts seem to be missing for the entrepreneur looking to higher education for support.

This realization that as an educator in higher education, I was simply teaching people how to become more successful employees, led me to resign my faculty position and quit teaching in higher education. The interesting part of this reflection and the Motil (2015) research study was that as an entrepreneur, the work / life balance vanishes. The entrepreneur no longer trades something they may hate doing to make a living (work) for something they LOVE doing, which is passion for the work, becoming a more effective home life (Charfen, 2015).

In leaving the traditional job as an employee role behind, I work doing something I love using these experiences to leverage additional experiences. The process becomes seemingly much easier when extracting the concept of the word *work* in the traditional sense. An integration exists that takes place between work life and home life (Charfen, 2015). There is also a complete parallel that takes place in the realization that the better one does at work; the stronger things tend to happen at home (Charfen, 2015).

The entrepreneur does not have the ability to turn off work because of their passion. A constant struggle exists of the things one loves to do and the things one also enjoys doing without being paid. Subsequently, there becomes a very interesting balance as work / life balance disappears (Charfen, 2015). Life balance takes its place as the struggle transforms trading things life requires vs.

things one loves to do, negating the stress relationship that many manage (Motil, 2017).

The Maslach Burnout Inventory (1981) focused on emotional exhaustion, cynicism, and reduced personal efficacy as part of the burnout/stress experience in search of work life balance. The emotional exhaustion comes from a stressful experience, when one is not doing something out of love (Chan, Leung, & Yuan, 2014; Devi & Kiran, 2014; Dhar, 2011; Ding, Ng, Wang, & Zou, 2012; Duke, Bergmann, Cunradi, & Ames, 2013; Lee, Jin, & Park, 2012; Leung, Bowen, Liang, & Famakin, 2015; Leung et al., 2015). Reduced personal efficacy is feeling the lack of purpose or fulfillment, participating in work that does not matter (Maslach, 1981). Being an entrepreneur eliminates this lack of purpose; passion drives engagement and purpose.

Lessons learned are many. An entrepreneur who chases money will ultimately fail, because of the level of difficulty (Motil, 2017). Especially when starting a new business with trying to grow a team, stress increases will get very difficult. An interesting note here is that although stress remains, the type of stress and purpose changes, fueling the desire to move forward (Kiyosaki & Lechter, 1997). The stress can be crushing at times, but those two sides of the burnout phenomenon disappear as stress is a different experience than the way an employee perceives working for somebody else in a job that highlights the loss of taking away from things that they would much rather being doing than doing whatever it is to get paid (Motil, 2017). As an employee, one trades their time for somebody else's money (Kiyosaki & Letcher, 1997). For the successful entrepreneur, one learns how to monetize their passion, reshaping the work / life balance equation. A different structure emerges that unravels the inner workings of the work / life balance, replacing the stress experience with a more positive outcome (Motil, 2017). A paradigm shift occurs when one transitions from employee to entrepreneur. The push and pull of work / life balance is replaced by balancing life in general. The entrepreneur's work life and home life become completely integrated (Charfen, 2015).

Disarming the Middle-Class Trap

The path to disarming the middle-class trap lies with the entrepreneurial personality type. The realization that the *American Dream* fed to the youth of America since the 1970s is a trap and there is a large group of people waking up to this truth. The problem becomes what to do once the realization is made. The entrepreneur in each of us needs to be awakened and rallied to action. America is the land of opportunity and those born and raised here were so incredibly quick to squander that opportunity the day we stepped foot onto the local college or university. Not that one could not leave the higher education system and pursue their dream, but this is not what we teach students to do! College and university students include training to be excellent employees, not independent thinkers, and certainly not captains of industry.

The lessons learned came from the work life balance equation begging a personal reflection of passion and purpose. One must closely examine life and work-related goals to decide whether to be a good employee or a successful business owner and entrepreneur. A refractive thinking approach demands thinking beyond the box to define a new set of rules beyond simply and only learning to be a good employee. One does not have to settle for traditional cultural expectations of following a path to college or to the trades where becoming an employee is the only option. As a former faculty and adult learner / student in higher education, an additional choice exists to become an entrepreneur and business owner. Students have realistic expectations to have faculty who understand and support more than simply learning to be a good employee. Entrepreneurial classes need to be taught by faculty who are entrepreneurs, who have their own businesses, those who created organizations beyond a sole proprietorship.

When I was a college student, I read the book *Rich Dad, Poor Dad* by Robert Kiyosaki (1997). The Rich Dad book was a wake-up call for me that the traditional path of employment was not the goal to creating the life and lifestyle I wanted for myself and eventually for my future family. The concept of creating wealth through investing in real estate fascinated me. I read every book written by Robert Kiyosaki to gain as much theoretical knowledge about real estate investing as possible. I did not understand the concept that one could begin a career in real estate investing without having money of their own; I believed I needed to finish my engineering degree and use money from my job to invest. Every time life got hard or stressful, I would put real estate on hold, so I could focus on my career; on what I was told I was *supposed* to do. I put my dream on hold because that is what I had been *trained* to do.

After a few years of focusing on my passion as a side project, I purchased enough real estate to where the passive income from rentals surpassed my monthly expenses at home. While I was still in debt with mortgages, children, car payments, student loans, credit cards and medical bills; I created a perpetual income through investing to cover all those expenses monthly without a lot of effort. I wrote the best-selling book *Man on Fire: Lessons from a Perpetual Burnout on Creating Alignment for Success* to help others follow the path I pursued to leverage real estate investing to disarm the middle-class trap, and fire their bosses forever (Motil, 2017).

The entrepreneur lives life on their own terms and they make their own rules. Living life on your own terms does not come without stress. The entrepreneur becomes completely responsible for success and failure on all levels; especially in a new start-up opportunity or organization. The level of responsibility increases after hiring employees. Through stress, the entrepreneur can evaluate and creatively adapt. Refractive thinking is critical for the entrepreneur. After making the jump to full-time entrepreneur, I personally learned is that one does not need to be the one purchasing the real estate to benefit either. Many options exist within the real estate world regarding the concept of leverage; to leverage (a) incomes, (b) retirement accounts, (c) savings, and (d) other people's money to invest passively as private lenders. Private lenders receive high yields on investments secured by the real estate without the active involvement of managing the assets. Only after many rounds of attempting success, failing, modifying actions, and trying again does the entrepreneur succeed. The overarching lesson is that one has options, many options rarely if ever within the traditional curriculum of higher education, consequently limiting the choices one may have to disrupt the circuitous cycle of a traditional path to success. The solution is to become a refractive thinker to learn about other options not often taught in school to live life under a different set of rules within your control and on your terms.

THOUGHTS FROM THE ACADEMIC ENTREPRENEUR

The problem to be solved:

- Successful integration of work and life balance as an entrepreneur.

The goals:

- To integrate emerging research about burnout and stress as an integral part of the entrepreneurial experience using the refractive thinking approach to examine why.

The question to ask:

- How can entrepreneurs work longer hours than traditional employees but avoid the burnout phenomenon?

Today's Business Application:

- Current academic research focuses on work/life balance from perspective of employer and employee and gaps exist for the entrepreneur.
- Entrepreneurs working in their passion have the ability to mitigate burnout.
- Employees can escape the burnout syndrome and middle class trap through entrepreneurship.

REFERENCES

Abbe, O. O., Harvey, C. M., Ikuma, L. H., & Aghazadeh, F. (2011). Modeling the relationship between occupational stressors, psychosocial / physical symptoms and injuries in the Construction Industry. *International Journal of Industrial Ergonomics, 41*, 106–117. doi:10.1016/j.ergon.2010.12.002

Alarcon, G. M. (2011). A meta-analysis of burnout with job demands, resources, and attitudes. *Journal of Vocational Behavior, 79*, 549–562. doi:10.1016/j.jvb.2011.03.007

An, S.-H., Zhang, Z., & Lee, U.-K. (2013). Correlation analysis between job stress and job satisfaction of building construction field managers. *Journal of the Korea Institute of Building Construction, 13*, 474–481. doi:10.5345/jkibc.2013.13.5.474

Bowen, P., Edwards, P., & Lingard, H. (2012). Workplace stress experienced by construction professionals in South Africa. *Journal of Construction Engineering and Management, 139*, 393–403. doi:10.1061/(ASCE)CO.1943-7862.0000625

Bowen, P., Edwards, P., & Lingard, H. (2013). Workplace stress among construction professionals in South Africa: The role of harassment and discrimination. *Engineering, Construction, and Architectural Management, 20*, 620–635. doi:10.1108/ECAM-05-2012-0051

Bowen, P., Edwards, P., Lingard, H., & Cattell, K. (2013). Predictive modeling of workplace stress among construction professionals. *Journal of Construction Engineering and Management, 140*(3). doi:10.1061/(ASCE)CO.1943-7862.0000806

Bowen, P., Edwards, P., Lingard, H., & Cattell, K. (2014). Occupational stress and job demand, control and support factors among construction project consultants. *International Journal of Project Management, 32*, 1273–1284. doi:10.1016/j.ijproman.2014.01.008

Bria, M., Spânu, F., Băban, A., & Dumitraşcu, D. L. (2014). Maslach Burnout Inventory–General Survey: Factorial validity and invariance among Romanian healthcare professionals. *Burnout Research, 1*, 103–111. doi:10.1016/j.burn.2014.09.001

Chan, I. Y., Leung, M., & Yuan, T. (2014). Structural relationships between cultural values and coping behaviors of professionals in the stressful construction industry. *Engineering, Construction and Architectural Management, 21*, 133–151. doi:10.1108/ECAM-07-2012-0069

Charfen, A. (2015). *The entrepreneurial personality type.* Austin, TX: The Charfen Institute.

Collins, J. (2001). *Good to great: Why some companies make the leap . . . and others don't.* New York, NY: HarperCollins.

Devi, K., & Kiran, U. V. (2014). Work life balance of women workers in construction industry. *European Academic Research, 2*, 4932–4946.

Dhar, R. L. (2011). Leisure as a way of coping with stress: An ethnographic study of the low-income construction workers. *Leisure, 35,* 339–360. doi:10.1080/149 27713.2011.614842

Ding, Z., Ng, F., Wang, J., & Zou, L. (2012). Distinction between team-based self-esteem and company-based self-esteem in the construction industry. *Journal of Construction Engineering and Management, 138,* 1212–1219. doi:10.1061/ (ASCE)CO.1943-7862.0000534

Duke, M. R., Bergmann, L., Cunradi, C. B., & Ames, G. M. (2013). Like swallowing a butcher knife: Layoffs, masculinity, and couple conflict in the United States construction industry. *Human Organization, 72*(4), 293–297, 300–301.

Kiyosaki, R. T., Lechter, S. T. (1997). *Rich dad, poor dad: What the rich teach their kids about money – that the poor and middle class do not!* New York, NY: Warner Books

Lee, H.-S., Jin, F.-J., & Park, M.-S. (2012). A study on factors influencing turnover intention of new employees in construction company. *Korean Journal of Construction Engineering and Management, 13,* 137–146. doi:10.6106/ KJCEM.2012.13.2.136

Leung, M., Bowen, P., Liang, Q., & Famakin, I. (2015). Development of a job-stress model for construction professionals in South Africa and Hong Kong. *Journal of Construction Engineering and Management, 141*(2), 04014077. doi:10.1061/(ASCE)CO.1943-7862.0000934

Lingard, H., Francis, V., & Turner, M. (2012). Work time demands, work time control and supervisor support in the Australian construction industry: An analysis of work-family interaction. *Engineering, Construction and Architectural Management, 19,* 647–665. doi:10.1108/09699981211277559

Lorente, L., Salanova, M., Martínez, I. M., & Vera, M. (2014). How personal resources predict work engagement and self-rated performance among construction workers: A social cognitive perspective. *International Journal of Psychology, 49,* 200–207. doi:10.1002/ijop.12049

Maslach, C., & Jackson, S. (1981). The measurement of experienced burnout. *Journal of Organizational Behavior, 2,* 99–113. doi:10.1002/job.4030020205

Maslach, C., Schaufeli, W., & Leiter, M. (2001). Job burnout. *Annual Review of Psychology, 52,* 397–422. doi:10.1146/annurev.psych.52.1.397

Maslow, A. (1954). *Motivation and personality* (3rd ed.). New York, NY: Harper & Row.

Mostert, K. (2011). Job characteristics, work–home interference and burnout: testing a structural model in the South African context. *The International Journal of Human Resource Management, 22,* 1036–1053. doi:10.1080/09585192.2011 .556777

Mostert, K., Peeters, M., & Rost, I. (2011). Work–home interference and the relationship with job characteristics and well-being: a South African study among employees in the construction industry. *Stress and Health*, *27*, 238–251. doi:10.1002/smi.1374

Motil, M. (2017). *Man on fire: Lessons from a perpetual burnout on creating alignment for success.* Cleveland, OH: Dr. Matt Motil.

Pinto, J. K., Dawood, S., & Pinto, M. B. (2014). Project management and burn-out: Implications of the demand–control–support model on project-based work. *International Journal of Project Management*, *32*, 578–589. doi:10.1016/j.ijproman.2013.09.003

Schaufeli, W., Leiter, M., Maslach, C., & Jackson, S. (1996). *MBI-General Survey* (3rd ed.). Palo Alto, CA: Consulting Psychologists Press.

Shen, Y., Tuuli, M. M., Xia, B., Koh, T. Y., & Rowlinson, S. (2014). Toward a model for forming psychological safety climate in construction project management. *International Journal of Project Management*. doi:10.1016/j.ijproman.2014.04.009

Small Business Administration (SBA). (2012). *Frequently asked questions.* Retrieved from https://www.sba.gov/sites/default/files/FAQ_Sept_2012.pdf

Turner, M., & Lingard, H. (2014). Identification and verification of demands and resources within a work–life fit framework: Evidence from the Australian construction industry. *Community, Work, & Family*, *17*, 1–20. doi:10.1080/13668 803.2014.933773

Xie, C., Wu, D., Luo, J., & Hu, X. (2010). A case study of multi-team communications in construction design under supply chain partnering. *Supply Chain Management*, *15*, 363–370. doi:10.1108/13598541011068279

Zhang, Z., Lee, W. H., Choi, Y.-W., & An, S. H. (2013). A comparative analysis of job stress of field managers and workers in Korean construction projects. *Journal of Building Construction and Planning Research*, *1*, 55–60. doi:10.4236/jbcpr.2013.13008

About the Author...

 Northeast Ohio author Dr. Matt Motil resides in North Olmsted, Ohio in the western suburbs of Cleveland with his wife, Amy, and their five children. He holds several accredited degrees: a Bachelor of Science (BS) in Mechanical Enigneering from the University of Toledo; a Master's of Business Administration (MBA) in project management from Ottawa University; and a Doctor of Business Administration (DBA) from Walden University. He is also a registered Professional Engineer (PE) in Arizona and Ohio.

Dr. Matt is a real estate entrepreneur, best-selling author, and host of The Cashflow King Podcast. He has worked with hundreds of investors from all over the world and helped them to grow massive wealth and passive income through remote real estate investments. After spending almost 20 years in the construction industry starting as a union laborer, working his way up to senior project management, he escaped the middle-class trap, utilizing rental real estate. Dr. Matt stopped teaching higher education when he realized he was simply helping people become better employees and now teaches people how to do exactly what he did, leverage real estate investing to fire their bosses forever!

To reach Dr. Matt Motil for information on real estate investing, mentorship, or guest speaking, please visit his websites: www.DrMattMotil.com or e-mail: matt@drmattmotil.com

CHAPTER 9

Entrepreneur! Really?

Dr. Les Paull

Often, one hears a word that stretches our lexicon and just as often that word morphs into multiple meanings, or perhaps one may simply not understand the full significance of the word at all. This is such a case here. The word *entrepreneur* includes broad application to anyone who is in business or who has an idea for one. Really? The Business Dictionary (2017) specifically defined an entrepreneur as

> . . . someone who exercises initiative by organizing a venture to take benefit of an opportunity and, as the decision maker, decides what, how, and how much of a good or service to produce. The entrepreneur is usually a sole proprietor, a partner, or the one who owns the majority of shares in an incorporated venture. (para. 1)

Although this definition includes identification of *some* of the elements of an entrepreneur; this definition misses others that equally apply. The object of this chapter is to provide qualitative and quantitative information to allow aspiring entrepreneurs to know what characteristics and experiences allow one to be called an entrepreneur. Perhaps these experiences may help those to understand this concept more fully to go beyond traditional understanding to find success in their world.

Experienced entrepreneurs will recognize the essential qualities described in this chapter and appreciate this more comprehensive definition of the term *entrepreneur*. Those anticipating becoming

155

entrepreneurs may gain insight into the numerous elements of entrepreneurship. While some scholars may question the depth of this understanding of entrepreneurship, it has been my experience that few writers of scholarly works about entrepreneurship have ever *been* entrepreneurs. Those who attempt to define the term *entrepreneur* typically use a qualitative method, *observing* active entrepreneurs, but few have any personal entrepreneurial experience, therefore, offering an incomplete understanding at best. When someone claims to be an entrepreneur, one should ask if he or she has actually experience in starting a company, if one fully understands riding the emotional and financial roller coaster of running a company, spent every waking hour working to keep the company alive, and then watched the company succeed—or fail—financially. The paragraphs that follow will offer a refractive thinking perspective that digs deep beyond the surface to explore the many challenges faced by the entrepreneur to offer inspiration and hope to anyone aspiring to such.

The Problem Is Understanding the Term *Entrepreneur*

In any field, an understanding based on *observation* is very different from an understanding based on actual personal experience. A sports writer may observe the sweat and strain of a tennis player in a professional match. He or she may be able to *imagine* what it feels like to play competitive tennis at a high level, but only one who has *played* the game is fully able to understand the focus, the inner thoughts, the sorrows and joys, the agony of defeat, and the ecstasy of victory. The same applies to those who write about entrepreneurs based on observation without personal experience. This chapter provides several personal scenarios that demonstrate the multiple ingredients necessary to be a genuine entrepreneur. The goal is to take the reader on a journey through the details of several personal real life entrepreneurial experiences to add to what many think they may understand.

To understand the term entrepreneur, one must attempt to understand the psyche of an entrepreneur (Carland, Carland, & Stewart, 2015). The goal is that these real-life stories may resonate and offer insight into the psyche of at least one entrepreneur. Each of the several businesses I started is both a blessing and a curse. Starting a business, keeping it running, and moving to profitability requires tremendous sacrifice. The amount of time, energy, and money necessary to start, operate, and move to profitability is often underestimated as a result of this lack of true understanding. One must be prepared to accept the enormous burden necessary to attain success. One's support network is essential to the owner, as well as the rest of the company. Many forget work life balance and the need to make time to be with family as this process unfolds, because the business has an increased probability of success when family is part of the journey (Fernández-Aráoz, Igbal, & Ritter, 2015).

Many make the assumption that business education is a significant factor in entrepreneurial success. However, as Bae, Qian, Miao, and Fiet (2014) suggested, little correlation exists between entrepreneurial *intentions* and business *education* within academia. It is important to grasp this lack of correlation, supported by my earliest experience as an entrepreneur. To understand this point further, one must delve into the mindset of those who become an entrepreneur.

The psyche of an entrepreneur is much like that of the number one pick in the NFL. How often do the scouts get it wrong? Quite often! According to Koz, Fraser-Thomas, and Baker, (2011), "a significant negative relationship between draft round and games played" (Abstract). Statistics and academic degrees may not reveal much about the drive, determination, and problem-solving ability of either the football player or fledgling entrepreneur. One must dig deeper into examining what lies beyond.

The foundation of an entrepreenuer requires a focus into their background to review the tools in their toolbox that may help lead toward success. In my case, educational experiences includes an undergraduate degree with a background in chemistry. On the surface, the reader may question the relevance of including this background as part of this discussion. This background is important because of the critical and refractive thinking skills a chemist must possess. A chemist constantly questions how and why things react to form new products (Tomlinson, 2013). Similarly, these skills transfer to the entrepreneur to focus on how and why a business solution might fit into a specific market segment and probable financial outcomes. The mindset of an entrepreneurmay may be far more important than simply one's academic background (Tomlinson, 2013).

A Sporting Proposition

Little did I know that my first major entrepreneurial experience would arise from my academic experience regarding teaching and coaching. I received a job offer to teach chemistry and coach the tennis team at a small military college in New Mexico. During the interview, *salesmanship* came into play when asked how I could benefit the college because of my experience. I replied my goal was to bring a national tennis championship to the school; a bold claim given that the school won only one match the previous year. Recruiting collegiate tennis players to a military college was a *marketing* and *sales* challenge which I had yet experienced up to that point in my career. Although I certainly had no formal education in those areas, I did have a *vision.* Yet another intangible skill important to the mindset of an entrepreneur. Brush (2013) argued that "to *learn* entrepreneurship, one must *do* entrepreneurship" (para. 4).

Most business people would agree that entrepreneurship starts with a *vision* and a *dream* that must manifest in products or services to become a business. My business charter included recruiting tennis players to play at the toughest junior college level in the United States. What I lacked in business education was made up for with a hard-wired competitive spirit, desire to succeed, and believe that nothing is impossible. Moreover, as Bae et al. (2014) found, no correlation exists between business education and success as an entrepreneur.

My vision for making my dream a reality was to deploy a marketing plan and implement that plan quickly, to deliver a quality product within 24 months. My first step into marketing involved learning how to sell a product that was stigmatized by adverse publicity. The Vietnam War was on, enrollment at all military colleges was down, and recruiting would be challenging. Although I did not yet know the term, these experiences were an introduction to the concept of *spillover risk*—adverse impacts in one company spilling over to other related companies (Beisswingert, Zhang, Goertz, & Fishbacher, 2016). Spillover risk must be understood to adequately assess the risks associated with any business model.

Because of this success, I became the chief executive officer (CEO) of a subsidiary of a parent organization, with control of an independent budget and staff, and the task of selling a service and delivering a product. My business plan quickly took shape with the implementation of a tactical marketing campaign to contact all the international tennis associations around the world, offering scholarships to their top tennis players. The ultimate goal was clear—to win tennis matches and bring honor to the college, which, in more than 100 years of educational success, even with the likes of Roger Staubach playing football for the college, had never won a national championship in any sport to date.

Keep in mind that my formal education was not in business; I was a scientist (chemistry) and a teacher (academia) (Tomlinson,

2013). After a full year of diligent work, my marketing and sales campaign began to pay off. To my amazement, the second year of marketing resulted in commitments from the number one tennis players from Japan, Bolivia, and Colombia, as well as three, ranked junior players from the United States. The biggest surprise of the business plan came during the third year of my tenure as an assistant professor and CEO of the tennis program. At the end of the third year of my business plan, the New Mexico (NM) Military Institute college tennis team won the NJCAA National Collegiate Tennis Championships, three of the players included selection as All-Americans, and I was personally honored as the National Junior CollegeTennis Coach of the Year. A burning desire to succeed regardless of any financial gain was the driving force behind the achievement of this goal, forming my foundation for business that came in later years.

Lessons Learned

A need for the emerging entrepreneur is to develop a business plan that links to a marketing and sales plan. Most entrepreneurs intend to operate a business for financial gain. Creating a strong business plan can bring focus and clarity that will result in increased financial success. The lessons learned include the need to be tactical about marketing to assure targeting the right segment of the market to meet the goals of the plan. Additionally, always be aware of the potential risks associated with failure, including spillover risk. The lesson is not to focus on financial success. Instead, ensure to concentrate on being successful at marketing and sales—the foundation of the entrepreneur mindset that includes critical and refractive thinking at its core (Beisswingert, Zhang, Goertz, & Fishbacher, 2016; Tomlinson, 2013).

Entrepreneurship comes in many forms, with many ingredients necessary to increase the probability of success. Though the rewards of coaching a national college tennis team were not monetary, the experience proved to be a phenomenal stepping-stone for my entrepreneurial career. I learned to not fear the unknown, there are those that will show the way. "Do not go where the path may lead, go instead where there is no path and leave a trail— Ralph Waldo Emerson." (Think Exist, 2017). Never give up the dream. Put passion into the vision and allow that emotion to flow to all in the project.

Drilling Deep

Willingness to take on new challenges with a flexible mind set helped facilitate growth as an entrepreneur. During my teaching and coaching career, I completed my MBA, with a finance emphasis. A chance meeting with Bert Murphy, CEO of Murphy Oil and Gas opened the door to more entrepreneurial experiences. Murphy became an influencial mentor who guided my growth as a businessman and person. After our first meeting and presentation of a marketing plan to sell the companies drillable oil and gas leases Murphy offered the position of Vice President of Marketing and Sales. Upon hire, I had complete autonomy to convert an inventory of millions of dollars' worth of drillable oil and gas leases into drilling projects and market and sell those projects to drilling partners, further increasing my skills and mindset of the nature of my role as an entrepreneur.

The first task was to implement the marketing plan that had landed me the job. The objective was to market and sell the drilling projects to other major oil exploration companies, reduce the inventory, and increase the cash flow, and revenue. Sale of certain leases would allow Murphy Oil and Gas to retain an overriding royalty interest, with me retaining a portion for all successful producing wells. I decided to package every project in the same format so that each presentation had the same sequence of events regardless of whom viewed the data and presentation. Maps of the leases, geologic data, reserve analysis, and the potential return on investment (ROI) were included in the package and always presented in the same sequence. Sales acumen and knowledge of the product are critical qualities for every entrepreneur (Tomlinson, 2013).

Remember, as listed in the introduction, The Business Dictionary (2017) included the description of an entrepreneur as "someone who exercises initiative by organizing a venture to take benefit of an opportunity and, as the decision maker decides what, how, and how much of a good or service to produce" (para. 1). This definition accurately described this new position because of the need for reliance on personal initiative, a specific vision and a dream, the ability to organize the venture, and the need to take advantage of the opportunity. However, one major challenge existed: my job had a performance clause that allowed just 6 months to prove the marketing plan and generate revenue. This *pay-for-performance model* is often part of the entrepreneur mindset, adding opportunity to work on additional skills.

After 3 months of packaging the inventory, I commenced the tactical marketing campaign. I sent a summary page of all the projects to 200 oil and gas CEOs in the United States. I had no fear of contacting the top executives at the largest oil companies operating in the United States. This experience reinforced the need that an entrepreneur should not fear rejection when reaching out to share an idea that will be beneficial to others. However, I did have some fear that my efforts would not be successful within the months allotted, and that I would soon be out of a job. Entrepreneurs often face uncertainty at the core of any business venture as there are no guarantees. Passion and a desire to see must be cultivated as part of the entrepreneurial skill set.

Within weeks of launching the marketing campaign, requests for more information started to arrive. With each request for information about the drillable prospects, it became apparent of the need to personally present the projects to each company, thus guaranteeing the homogeneity of the presentations. My presentation technique focused on the science of the project, and the potential *ROI* each project offered, but I also infused a personal understanding of each project, enthusiasm for the projects, a passion for answering the prospects' questions, and gratitude for their time to allow the presentations—all elements of the entrepreneur and the desire to succeed at all costs (Beisswingert, Zhang, Goertz, & Fishbacher, 2016).

During the next 3 months, I crisscrossed the Southwest United States making presentations to all the major and independent oil and gas exploration companies I could meet in person (perhaps this element remains at the heart of business—being able to look someone in the eye and shake their hand as part of building a busieness relationship). As the 6 month deadline for proving my marketing sales concept approached, the marketing and sales efforts had not produced any revenue. A feeling of doom and gloom abounded.

Dreading the loss of my job, I had to attend a prescribed 6-month meeting with Murphy to discuss whether my job remained. I will never forget Murphy's tone, body language, and demeanor as my insides were shaking in anticipation I failed and would soon be terminated. Murphy showed me that the quality of being a good leader and entrepreneur does not always mean immediate success, but can be a patient attitude and belief in the system and individual or individuals operating the system (B. Murphy, personal communication, 1982). Those lessons of that day carried forward and passed on many times to others in my employ. My tenure at Murphy Oil and Gas extended through the end of the year, as Murphy commented about my commitment to the task, innovative approach, hard work, and perseverance. He said that he believed in me and the system as well as the process. Then he wished me continued success and full speed ahead. Another lesson here is the power of an affirmation to provide increased motivation to succeed.

My limited previous entrepreneurial experience combined with a phenomenal mentor yielded far better results than envisioned. From the seventh month of employment, revenue and sales mounted steadily, continuing through the balance of the year. Laser focus on the task of marketing and selling oil and gas projects produced a significant number of sales, significant revenue, and profits for the company, and, for myself, financial reward and promotion to President of the company. Laser focus—another entrepreneurial quality that requires cultivation. Murphy provided me a unique opportunity, a challenge that my formal education and training had not qualified me for, and yet my fledgling entrepreneurial experience, a well-planned approach to the challenge, and a lot of determination and focus produced results beyond all expectations. I pondered then, as I have many times over my career, the age-old question, "Does the man make the times, or do the times make the man" (Anonymous, n.d.).

Lessons Learned

One can be an entrepreneur within an operating organization and experience all the benefits, joys, and frustrations without launching a startup business. This distinction is important as a business owner may not be an entrepreneur by definition and an entrepreneur does not imply being a business owner. For an entrepreneur, the importance exists to become as personally involved with all aspects of the organization as possible. Commit mind, body, and spirit, to completing the task at hand through hard work and dedication. Never stop using an innovative mind to bring about new thoughts, ideas, and concepts. Persevere through the tough times using inner strength that compelled the original vision and desire. Focus on successfully finishing each task rather than on the potential financial gain. If one achieves success at the task, the financial gains will follow.

Lean and Green

An accepted axiom of business says that *necessity is the mother of invention* ("Necessity is the," 2017). The following demonstrates why the axiom is true. After many years with Murphy, I formed Paull Petroleum Corporation (PPC) to explore for oil and gas reserves. Success came easy for the first 5 years of operations. The company drilled and operated more than 200 productive wells, with more than 100 people employed. The financial needs of the company and my family were secure, allowing an experience of self-actualization as described by Carland et al. (2015) stating that many business people receive self-actualization from their work.

Carland et al. (2015) observed that business owners with relatively low entrepreneurial drive viewed their firms as vehicles for providing basic financial needs, while those with higher entrepreneurial drive viewed their businesses as vehicles for achieving self-esteem and actualization. I saw myself in the latter category, absolutely certain that success would continue forever. However, forever suddenly came to a screeching halt. An abrupt drop in oil prices from $32 per barrel to $9 per barrel, in 1999 created a huge cash flow shortfall for the company and my family.

During the 6 months after the oil market crash, I struggled to keep the employees working and the company afloat, but finally was forced to choose between closing the company and filing bankruptcy. The entrepreneurial success of the past 10 years was suddenly gone, finances were at a minimum, and survival was my new mission. At this juncture in life, it became apparent that being an entrepreneur is not determined by a single experience or a few successful ventures, but rather a mindset that awakens to challenges and new opportunities in good and bad times.

The closing of my company left me with two choices: cry and feel sorry for myself or pick up the pieces and find a new horizon. A true entrepreneur is not bound by a single successful idea or a company's success or failure. As an avid student of innovative technologies, I happened across an article about a new personal office laser printer that was coming to market. The technology intrigued me enough to research how and why this technology would be beneficial to the personal office work environment. Prudent research led me to conclude that the laser printer was here to stay and that there was a possible niche business if I could solve the problem of toner leaking from the cartridges and develop a method to recycle high-quality cartridges. A vision began to take shape—a vision that expanded to include laser cartridges that no longer leaked, landfills free of unnecessary plastic, metal, and toner waste, and a new business training people to recycle the cartridges and create their individual independent, socially responsible business.

These events found me experimenting in my basement, searching for a sealing system that would remedy the leaking toner problem. While working on the sealing system, I read an article in the local newspaper about a startup company that was remanufacturing laser printer cartridges. The recycled cartridges were cleaned and replenished with toner. The term recycled lacked in a significant area, a quality equal to or better than the original equipment manufacturing (OEM). After investigating this company, I decided that purchasing was a faster way to get into the market than starting a new company. After purchasing the organization, I completed an innovative sealing system which stopped toner leakage, patented the design, and began utilizing the technology to provide cartridges that exceeded the OEM. To provide a new innovative product as a recycled replacement, the recycled cartridges had to meet or exceed the original equipment manufacturer (OEM) specifications. After confirming that our recycled cartridges exceeded OEM standards, focus shifted to the total vision of starting a new industry, training people to recycle laser printer cartridges.

My tactical marketing plan was designed to determine the level of interest of individuals willing to buy a select area license to produce and sell recycled laser printer cartridges, an opportunity that required little capital and offered the potential for excellent returns. Ads in various magazines offering licensing and training opportunities provided the introduction to a new innovative business opportunity. Within 90 days, 20 to 30 requests a week came in from the United States and international people interested in attending training classes, paying a license fee, and receiving new proprietary products developed simultaneously with the sealing system.

Because of personal impending doom and gloom, necessity motivated the invention of new technology. The ability to draw on previous entrepreneurial experience and knowledge provided a platform to launch a global cottage industry. Proudly, the recycling of laser printer cartridges was responsible for recycling more than 35 million cartridges in the United States at year-end 2015. While my patent rights and innovative dreams have long since become public domain, I remain satisfied, knowing that recycling of printer cartridges continues and that the landfills are being spared millions of pounds of plastic, metal, and toner waste from laser printer cartridges.

Lessons Learned

The upward trend of successful entrepreneurship does not always continue as planned. An entrepreneur must believe in him or herself in good times and bad. As the saying goes, "If at first, you do not succeed, try, try again." According to Decker, Haltiwanger, Jarmin, and Miranda (2014), "most business startups exit within their first 10 years, and most surviving young businesses do not grow but remain small. Furthermore, business start-ups account for about 20% of U.S. gross (total) job creation" (p. 10). Persistence is key to success.

Call on past experiences for use in new ways for new objectives. Do not let a failure or series of failures stop the flow of dreams for business innovation. Look at all of the components currently used in a market then use those elements in a realigned capacity to produce greater efficiencies or innovation that replaces the existing product or service. It is not necessary to reinvent the wheel or start a new business. Make a better wheel and success follows. Perhaps the best expression of entrepreneurship is that suggested by Chell, Spence, Perrini, and Harris (2016), stating, "Over the past decade, governments, academics, and practitioners have begun to place greater emphasis on *social* entrepreneurship" (p. 5). If all businesses emphasized social responsibility, our world would be a better place. Recycling laser printer cartridges proved to be a socially responsible business, yet it was also a financially prosperous business. Social responsibility and profitability are not mutually exclusive. Go forth, young entrepreneurs!

Conclusion

Entrepreneur! Really? Many components exist regarding being an entrepreneur, making it impossible to provide a short definition. Certainly, an entrepreneur must have a vision, be willing to take risks, and work long hours. As the above examples demonstrate refractive thinking, it is not necessary for an entrepreneur to be in a traditional business setting or to start a company. An emerging trend is for young people with business degrees or in business in any form, to identify themselves as entrepreneurs. Most should, at best, consider themselves *aspiring* entrepreneurs. Regardless of one's educational background or qualitative understanding of what makes an entrepreneur, until one successfully transforms an innovative idea into a successful business, invests one's entire being into making a dream a reality with blood, sweat, and tears to achieve profitability, one remains at best only an observer. Henderson Brower and Steward (2015) appropriately asked the question whether a role exists for classically trained professors in business schools of the future, suggesting that perhaps business faculty may simply need to go back to work. The next time someone states they are an entrepreneur perhaps the question to ask is: Really?

THOUGHTS FROM THE ACADEMIC ENTREPRENEUR

The problem to be solved:

- Provide a clearer understanding of the term entrepreneur

The goals:

- Allow aspiring entrepreneurs and authors with minimal or no entrepreneurial experience a better understanding of the components that determine an accurate description of an entrepreneur.

The questions to ask:

- Are you really an entrepreneur?
- Can you describe an entrepreneur having never been one?
- What are the essential ingredients to be an entrepreneur?

Today's Business Application:

- Too many business people use the word entrepreneur to describe what area of business they represent yet are clueless what entrepreneur engenders.
- Describing one's self as an entrepreneur should, at a minimum, be based on knowledge of what constitutes an entrepreneur.
- Comprehension of the ingredients necessary to be referred to as an entrepreneur will, at least, allow many aspiring entrepreneurs to distinguish what ingredients they possess (or not) to call themselves and entrepreneur.
- Authors who write about entrepreneurs and entrepreneurship are better served if they have experience as an entrepreneur.

REFERENCES

Business Dictionary. (2017). *Entrepreneur*. Retrieved from http://www.business-dictionary.com/

Bae, T. J., Qian, S., Miao, C., & Fiet, J. O. (2014). The relationship between entrepreneurship education and entrepreneurial intentions: A meta-analytic review. *Entrepreneurship Theory and Practice, 38*(2), 217-254. doi:10.1111/etap.12095

Beisswingert, B. Zhang, K., Goertz, T., & Fishbacher, U. (2016, March, 1). Spillover effects of loss of control on risky decision-making. *Plos Journal*. https://dx.doi.org/10.1371/journal.pone.0150470

Brush, C. (2013, September 1). *New ways to teach Entrepreneurship: A practice*. Retrieved from https://www.forbes.com/sites/babson/2013/09/21/new-way-to-teach-entrepreneurship-a-practice/#1ca58c4d24e8Carland, J. W., Carland, J. A. C., & Carland III, J. W. T. (2015). Self-actualization: The zenith of entrepreneurship. *Journal of Small Business Strategy, 6*(1), 53-66. Retrieved from http://libjournals.mtsu.edu/index.php/jsbs/article/view/306

Carland, J. C., Carland, J. W., & Stewart, W. H. (2015). Seeing what's not there: The enigma of entrepreneurship. *Journal of Small Business Strategy, 7*(1), 1-20. Retrieved from http://libjournals.mtsu.edu/index.php/jsbs/article/view/326

Carland, J. W., Carland, J. A. C., & Carland III, J. W. T. (2015). Self-actualization: The zenith of entrepreneurship. *Journal of Small Business Strategy, 6*(1), 53-66. Retrieved from http://libjournals.mtsu.edu/index.php/jsbs/article/view/306

Chell, E., Spence, L. J., Perrini, F., & Harris, J. D. (2016). Social entrepreneurship and business ethics: Does social equal ethical? *Journal of Business Ethics, 133*, 619-625. doi:10.1016/j.jbusvent.2013.05.001

Decker, R., Haltiwanger, J., Jarmin, R., & Miranda, J. (2014). The role of entrepreneurship in US job creation and economic dynamism. *The Journal of Economic Perspectives, 28*(3), 3-24. doi:10.1257/jep.28.3.3

Fernández-Aráoz, C., Igbal, S., & Ritter, J. (2015, April). Lessons learned from great family businesses. Harvard Business Review. Retrieved from https://hbr.org/2015/04/leadership-lessons-from-great-family-businesses

Henderson Brower, H., & Steward, M. D. (2015, November 27). Business professors need to spend time in companies. *Harvard Business Review*. Retrieved from https://hbr.org/2015/11/business-professors-need-to-spend-time-in-companies

Koz, D., Fraser-Thomas, J., & Baker, J. (2011, November 3). Accuracy of professional sports drafts in predicting career potential. *Scandinavian Journal of Medicine and Science in Sports*. doi:10.1111/j.1600-0838.2011.01408.x

Necessity is the mother of invention. (2017). Retrieved from http://www.invention-help.com/necessity-is-the-mother-of-invention

Think Exist. (2017). *Ralph Waldo Emerson*. Retrieved from http://thinkexist.com/ quotation/do_not_go_where_the_path_may_lead-go_instead/160119.html

Tomlinson, S. (2013, April 15). *Baroness Thatcher used her chemistry degree to tackle politics 'with the mindset of a scientist', says friend Dame Mary Archer*. Retrieved from. http://www.dailymail.co.uk/news/article-2309252/ Margaret-Thatcher-used-chemistry-degree-approach-politics-mindset-scientist-says-Mary-Archer.html

About the Author...

Dr. Les Paull holds a Bachelor of Arts in Chemistry from Linfield College, a Master of Business Administration (MBA) in Finance from Eastern New Mexico University, and a Doctor of Business Administration (DBA) in International Business from Walden University. Additionally, Dr. Les holds certificates in Petroleum Geology, Petroleum Finance, and Petroleum Engineering from the International Education and Development Department at the University of Oklahoma. He also holds coaching certificates from the U.S. Professional Teaching Association for Tennis and was honored as the U.S. National Junior College Tennis Coach of the Year. He holds U.S. patents for several of his inventions which are in commercial use in many parts of the world.

As an adjunct professor, Dr. Les taught Entrepreneurial Science at the University of Texas at Austin Graduate School of Business and Chemistry at Eastern NM University. As an assistant professor, he taught chemistry and math at the NM Military Institute while coaching both tennis and wrestling. Dr. Les is a frequent guest lecturer on entrepreneurship at many domestic and international seminars and conferences.

For the past 35 years, Dr. Les focused on mergers, acquisitions, and start-ups, having launched 10 of his own companies.

To reach Dr. Les Paull for information about entrepreneurship, starting companies, buying and selling organizations, or other related business functions, please email: profpaull@hotmail.com

CHAPTER 10

The Effectiveness of Teaching Entrepreneurship Programs in Higher Education

Dr. Neil Mathur & Dr. Cheryl Lentz

Faculty in higher education have an enormous challenge in attempting to teach what they do not know. While a bold statement, the topic continues to be debated in higher education entrepreneurship programs taught by management educators for past decades to date. If entrepreneurship drives the U.S. economy and those of countries around the world, and that higher education includes the responsibility of training the emerging and developing global work force and shaping the minds of future generations, the challenge becomes difficult when entrepreneurial students require *actual* experience from their teachers as part of their development in the classroom. Herein lies the problem—the lack among full and part-time / adjunct faculty of the appropriate business ownership and entrepreneurial experience—which are not the same thing—needed to fill this gap. For the mind of the entrepreneur, a traditional *train-the-trainer model* or *do-as-I-say-not-as-I-have-done model* fails miserably, often missing the mark entirely, as the entrepreneurial student experience lacks experiential context. The purpose of this chapter is to explore viable solutions to the question of who should teach this emerging population of *students as entrepreneurs,* as these minds impact the future of business and force an adjustment of the traditional teaching model in higher education. The purpose of this article is also to explore refractive thinking in the concepts of Peter Senge (1990), as new ideas cannot be put into old constructs. Instead, the refractive thinker must expand beyond this limited realm and follow Albert Einstein's (1954) assertion that one cannot use the same consciousness to solve a problem that created it. A Socratic thinker may ask *why,* while a refractive thinker asks *why not* or *what if,* which will be the focus of the argument that follows.

Who Shall Lead?

UNCTAD (2012) referred to the rise of the creative entrepreneur as those "able to transform ideas into creative products and services used to represent a new attitude and new way of thinking" (as cited in Dawson & Andriopoulus, 2017, p. 407). This definition is in contrast to the traditional academic for whom change does not happen quickly. For many people not actively involved in industry, this definition lacks contextual understanding that could add richness and experiential knowledge to the student experience. On the importance of learning, The Kaufman Foundation (2017) proposed, "If intelligibility is a fundamental goal of learning, then American higher education must reflect the experience and conditions of contemporary life. Higher education cannot make intelligible a world from which it is removed or does not address" (para. 2). If the future of America depends on small businesses and their owners, and if the minds of small business owners are in the hands of higher education, what are the institutions of higher learning in the United States (and globally) doing about finding the *right* people with the most effective knowledge and experience to teach this emerging group of students? Should higher education not be a mirror of experience to shape the future minds of these emerging risk takers, particularly because of their importance to global economies?

According to Rodov and Truong (2015),

. . . minorities own 15% of all U.S. businesses, accounting for $591 billion in revenues. (In addition), Women are starting businesses at one-and-a-half times the national average and currently own 40% of all businesses, producing nearly $1.3 trillion in revenues. (para. 7)

According to the GEM 2016–2017 Senior Entrepreneurship Report, 11% Young (18–29), 18% Middle age (30–49), 18% of seniors (50+) are self-employed. If these entrepreneurs represent this percentage of the total population, then the challenge for higher education is to give these groups of students reasons to attend institutions of higher learning amid a promise of what academics can teach future business owners and entrepreneurs.

If one looks to our friends to the north, 78% of Canada's one million businesses employ fewer than five people (Mathur, Flaschner, & Gill, 2011), supporting the importance of growing the future of *global* business beyond American borders. "One cannot ignore the individual difficult factors that affect negatively Canada's propensity to grow and expand business in Canada" (Mathur et al., 2011, p. 1). These factors include the knowledge of individual business owners and entrepreneurs who are part of this future growth supporting the need for this focus in business schools within higher education.

Small business drives the Canadian economy as well. Despite this knowledge, barriers to higher education still exist in Canada. Entrepreneurs need fundamental business skills to succeed. But with Canada's ultra-competitive graduate higher education programs, only top students gain acceptance into graduate programs (Mathur et al., 2011). This phenomenon gives rise to the irony of higher education in Canada. Those who already have business skills via an undergraduate degree may advance their skills through graduate university programs; however, those who lack business skills but wish to start a business cannot get accepted into the advanced training of a graduate business program (Mathur et al., 2011). With small business driving the economy, and new businesses failing at a high rate (Decker, Haltiwanger, Jarmin, & Miranda, 2014), most not surviving beyond 5 years, a paradox exists. Businesses fail, and the economy suffers because entrepreneurs cannot get the training they need because have no previous training in business.

The argument is more than simply the importance of education and the vast numbers of individuals who own businesses that will continue to shape the future of business. The emerging part of the argument is about who shall teach these students and within what medium. For those professors who have the entrepreneur calling, Phelan (2010) indicated that "Students see the passion we bring for science and entrepreneurship and it's easier for them to see themselves doing it too" (Levine, 2012, para. 24). In addition, Levine (2012) suggested that "Entrepreneurship activity invariably also helps scientists improve their ability to articulate concepts to numerous publics. . . "As you explain complicated scientific processes to different audiences," [says Phelan], "it makes you a better teacher and helps improve your critical thinking and communications skills" (para. 26). Thus, leading by example—by faculty participating in the process of entrepreneurship and business ownership—supports the need for a shift in the experience of faculty who teach.

Another barrier exists in using practitioner faculty, who are nontraditional academics, not paying their academic dues through research. Traditional academic institutions see professors as office-bound researchers who best exemplify real-world experience via complex research agendas. Even though research is undoubtedly a key component of academic currency, it often does not translate easily into entrepreneurship skills applicable to a local business owner. A chasm exists between academic learning and practical application. Academic institutions have often operated in a vacuum, creating research for one another, but often forgetting how to disseminate findings into actual tools that the average entrepreneur can learn on Monday and apply on Tuesday.

Should Professors Go Back to Work?

Perhaps the challenge is whether the pendulum has swung too far from the intention of business schools and their mission. According to Henderson Brower and Steward (2015) within the Harvard Business Review, because of the demand of economics and the desire to demonstrate a high return on investment for a degree in higher education, a closer inspection of the missions of business schools in particular, and the professors who teach in them is underway. Back in the 1950s, business schools received criticism for too much of a focus on applied education and vocational training. Business schools adjusted curriculum in response. In 2017, the criticism is for perhaps going too far the other direction. Warren Bennis, a renowned leadership scholar from the University of Southern California, stated that business schools have 'an overemphasis on the rigor and an under emphasis on relevance'" (Henderson Brower & Steward, 2015, para. 2).

Traditionally, teams of research-focused academics set the business curriculum through a predictable and flawed process. Accrediting bodies seek standardization of curriculum for conformity and comfortability of what they know. For an industry focused on constant research and new data, the process of accrediting curriculum is antiquated and static. The curriculum development process typically begins with minimal market analysis and maximum replication of existing programs to use a template that accreditors know and seek. Course curriculum is developed from a top-down approach of Deans, directors, and professors deciding what students should know. This approach creates a sound *academic* approach, but pays little attention to *industry voices* who eventually hire their students.

One potential model exists that bridges the gap between real-world practice and university research. Academic institutions currently research placement rates of alumni, but rarely invite industry to the curriculum-development table. Audience-analysis is a vital component of business communication skills taught in business schools; yet academic institutions rarely partake in this skill by asking themselves, *"What does the real world say we need to improve in our curriculum?"* A bottom-up model might help bridge the gap between theory and practice, integrate essential feedback from industry, and improve the business skills of potential business owners.

Wherein lies the solution? The Higher Education may return to practitioner faculty in hiring *professors of practice* or industry executives without PhDs going back to the basics of *you can't teach what you don't know.* Henderson Brower and Steward (2015) asked whether a role exists for classically trained professors in business schools of the future, suggesting business faculty may need to go back to work.

The problem is that less than 16% of academic in higher education own their own business (Shane, 2009). Clery and Lee (2002) pointed to their study to offer a beginning discussion about the expertise of current faculty in higher education.

In addition, 54% of full-time faculty members received income for activities out-side the institution, averaging eight hours per week. The average faculty member received $12,767 annually for this work; the data showed little variance among institutional types. Consulting was the most frequently reported source of outside income; 21% of full-time faculty members received income from this source. The range: 24% in public four-year institutions, 22% in private, not-for-profit institutions, and 14% in public two-year institutions. Full-time faculty members averaged $7,518 in consulting income. Less frequently reported sources of outside income included other academic institutions, self-owned businesses, and other employment. (Clery & Lee, 2002, p. 7)

Since the 1993 Kaufman index, "the share of new entrepreneurs who are college graduates increased from 23.7 to 33% (survey of 510, 689). This increase means that entrepreneurs are the largest educational category in the United States" (Clery & Lee, 2002, p. 6). As institutions of higher learning look to meet the needs of this emerging category of students, the challenge is to consider who should teach entrepreneurs, particularly regarding applicable expertise and experience in addition to their teaching credentials. Teaching entrepreneurs is not the same as teaching traditional college students with many programs steeped in the tradition of their disciplines' foundational theory. The entrepreneur, as well as the emerging entrepreneur student, requires new teaching methods.

Universities have an opportunity at the nexus between traditional academics and practitioner faculty. Historically, faculty practitioner work outside the university was discouraged and seen as a distraction for traditional teaching and research models. But some business entrepreneurship skills create an essential component of teaching–practitioner experience. Although students can learn theoretical application from professors sharing their research, real-world stories create a demonstrable application of learning to which students can relate.

The issue of taking traditional faculty out of the office and putting them into the real world emerges. The evaluation of faculty usually includes the review of teaching and research skills, but only a small element of their evaluation concerns outside activities. A lack of real-world entrepreneurial and business experience can create a barrier for traditional faculty to simply leave academics and transition into industry. Universities can change how they evaluate faculty by including criteria for faculty to serve in industry, such as serving on advisory boards, volunteering their expertise to improve local businesses.

This change creates a win-win situation for all stakeholders. Businesses gain valuable expertise and faculty obtain the important experience and real-world stories to bring to their classroom. Academic institutions create a communication channel between industry and academics, resulting in increased exposure and new potential enrolments

According to Rodov and Truong (2015),

> While society innovates, our K-12 schools have remained stagnant. As a result, they are not graduating the doers, makers and cutting-edge thinkers the world needs. Certainly, some public and private schools are modernizing—having students work in groups to solve problems, learn online and integrate science with the arts. But most institutions do not teach what should be the centerpiece of a contemporary education: entrepreneurship, the capacity to not only start companies but also to think creatively and ambitiously. (para. 1)

According to Brush (2013), several areas of focus regarding teaching entrepreneurship exist to include retention and enrollment of students,

> As students are being lured by the promise of success by dropping out, colleges and universities are working hard to show another side of the story – that there is value in staying in and launching a startup with the support of professors, mentors, and an innovation ecosystem. (para. 1)

In addition,

> As schools continue to battle for enrollments, and to differentiate themselves from their competitors, many schools have seen entrepreneurship as a key tool in attracting and retaining stu-

dents. They have also seen opportunities to create new revenue streams through licensing the intellectual property of researchers and scientists. (Brush, 2013, para. 3)

The challenge remains of the need for faculty to connect from theory to practical application. First-hand experience is needed and necessary to close this gap in knowledge acquisition and contextual understanding.

> Given the tremendous growth in the number of schools offering entrepreneurship courses, incubators, accelerators, and other vehicles to promote innovation by students and throughout the organization, it's no surprise that more student startups are taking their ideas to market. It's too early to tell whether these initiatives will be successful in retaining students who might otherwise drop out, but it's clear that entrepreneurship is the new core competency in higher education. (Brush, 2013, para. 3)

Brush presents an interesting irony to consider where forward thinking universities see the value of actual entrepreneurship practice in the classroom, traditional universities discourage entrepreneurial activities by claiming intellectual property of any new inventions from faculty. Where does the solution then lie?

Thus, the question is whether only faculty who have the experience of creating and owning their own business should be those to lead the educational experience and teaching of those who already have or who want to learn the mindset of the entrepreneur, which is not the same as that of a business owner. According to Rodov and Truong (2015),

> Entrepreneurship education benefits students from all socioeconomic backgrounds because it teaches kids to think outside the box and nurtures unconventional talents and skills. Furthermore, it creates opportunity, ensures social justice, instills confidence and stimulates the economy. (para. 3)

The popularity of entrepreneurial programs across the United States is a testament to the new need in higher education.

Between 1985 and 2008, the number of entrepreneurship courses in U.S. colleges and universities increased from 250 to over 5,000, and that number has continued to grow. Today, it's estimated that nearly half a million students are taking courses in entrepreneurship across the country. Colleges are making a concerted effort to convince these budding business owners that rather than dropping out they should stay in school and launch their ventures from inside the supportive ecosystem of their alma mater. (Tynan, 2015, para. 2)

While schools agree that losing their best and brightest to the startup economy is a problem, they are taking different approaches to solving the problem. For some schools, the answer lies in direct investment into startups by students. (Tynan, 2015, para. 3)

The debate continues regarding the most effective strategies to teach this emerging population.

The Debate Remains: Experience or Not?

The debate between traditional or ivory tower academics and non-traditional, outside-the-the box, refractive thinking academics remains.

For decades, we have debated whether entrepreneurship should be taught by entrepreneurs who have real world practical experience, or whether it should be taught from the perspective of theory, like other business disciplines. On the one hand, there are entrepreneurs telling war stories about how they achieved success with their insights and attributes. On the other hand, a more scholarly approach focuses on activity that involves the discovery, evaluation, and exploitation of opportunities to introduce new goods and services, ways of organizing, markets, process, and raw materials through organizing efforts that previously had not existed. Students, however, depending on their level and learning objectives, vary in the degree to which they need (and want) to see the theory. (Brush, 2013, para. 4)

We argue that in order to learn entrepreneurship, one must do entrepreneurship. But doing entrepreneurship definitely does not exclude theory. On the contrary, effective doing of entrepreneurship requires a set [of] practices and these practices are firmly grounded in theory. What is a practice and why is this the best approach? (Brush, 2013, para. 7)

Henderson Brower and Steward (2015) continue the debate arguing both sides of the argument. Could faculty be more effective with having some distance from business? Or is an outside experiential view from the inside offers a more expanded and broader perspective to encourage critical and refractive thinking? Perhaps a question to consider is not what is taught in business schools but rather what businesses are *actually practicing*? Perhaps the truth and the solution lies somewhere in between both of these extremes.

Business schools often end their graduate curriculum with students needing to prepare a report on how to improve a local business. Students must research a local company, possibly interviewing a business owner, and then writing a theoretical paper on how to improve the business. This theoretical approach creates a hypothetical assessment that caters to the strength of faculty who conventionally use assignment templates and rubrics to evaluate students. The problem of predictability and conformity arises here much like with accrediting bodies. The essence of higher education is to teach creativity and critical thinking skills that can apply to multiple situations, yet faculty assess students on the most convenient and standardized methods used.

Instead, business schools can require students to act as consultants who take their business solutions back to the local business, present their findings and develop a clear implementation plan for entrepreneurs and industry leaders. These presentations might humanize the theoretical application and create career opportunities for students to gain employment following completion of business curriculum. These presentations might also imply new opportunities for schools. Student alumni can attest that their business training helped them get gainful employment, which in turn enhances the prospects of new enrolments via student success stories. A bridge between theory and practice emerges and faculty would get valuable experience assessing application of student learning to the real world.

Conclusion

The debate will continue regarding the enormous challenge for academics in higher education in attempting to teach what it does not know from first experience. Is faculty with insider first-hand experience as a business owner and entrepreneur more valuable to the comprehensive and contextual student experience? The purpose of this chapter was to explore the question of who should teach this emerging population of *students as entrepreneurs,* as these minds impact the future of business and force an adjustment of the traditional teaching model in higher education. Our goal was to follow refractive thinking to ask *why not* or *what if,* regarding who is most effective to teach and train the future entrepreneurs of the future . . . perhaps the solution lies somewhere in the midst of these extremes.

THOUGHTS FROM THE ACADEMIC ENTREPRENEUR

The problem to be solved:

- Preparing for and managing higher education of the future global workforce

- Focusing on the need for theory and practitioner context for the student experience

The goals:

- Understanding the unique differences between traditional students and entrepreneurial students and their academic needs

- Understanding how to prepare student entrepreneurs and business owners for the challenges that lie ahead

The questions to ask:

- Is it more effective to have only faculty who own their own businesses teach entrepreneur classes?

- Who are the best faculty to train the entrepreneurs and business owners of the future?

Today's Business Application:

- Effective institutions of higher learning that understand the unique needs of the student entrepreneur mindset know how to effectively prepare student entrepreneurs of the future

- Preparation is fundamental to prevent or lessen the effects of ineffective university business programs.

- Use of practitioner faculty may prove to be a more effective model for preparing the global work force

REFERENCES

Brush, C. (2013, September 1). *New ways to teach Entrepreneurship: A practice.* Retrieved from https://www.forbes.com/sites/babson/2013/09/21/new-way-to-teach-entrepreneurship-a-practice/#1ca58c4d24e8

Brooks, R., Green, W. S., Hubbard, R. Glenn, J, D., Katehi, L., Mclendon, G., . . . & Roonkin, M. (2007). Entrepreneurship in American higher education. In Kauffman: The Foundation of Entrepreneurship. *A Report from the Kauffman Panel in Entrepreneurship Curriculum in Higher Education.*

Clery, S. B., & Lee, J. B. (2002). Faculty salaries: Recent trends. *The NEW 2002 Almanac of Higher Education.* Retrieved from http://www.nea.org/assets/img/PubAlmanac/ALM_02_03.pdf

Dawson, P., & Andriopolous, C. (2017). *Managing change, creativity, and innovation.* Thousand Oaks, CA: Sage.

Decker, R., Haltiwanger, J., Jarmin, R., & Miranda, J. (2014). The role of entrepreneurship in US job creation and economic dynamism. *The Journal of Economic Perspectives, 28*(3), 3-24. doi:10.1257/jep.28.3.3

Global Entrepreneurship Monitor (GEM). 2017). *Special topic report: 2016-2017 Senior entrepreneurship.* Retrieved from http://www.babson.edu/Academics/centers/blank-center/global-research/gem/Documents/GEM%202016-2017%20Senior%20Entrepreneurship.pdf

Henderson Brower, H., & Steward, M. D. (2015, November 27). Business professors need to spend time in companies. *Harvard Business Review.* Retrieved from https://hbr.org/2015/11/business-professors-need-to-spend-time-in-companies

Levine, A., G. (2012, September 14). Finding balance: The professor/entrepreneur. Retrieved from http://www.sciencemag.org/careers/features/2012/09/finding-balance-professorentrepreneur

Mathur, N., Flaschner, A., & Gill, A. (2011, June). *Growth plans of small business in Western Canada: Individual differences.* Paper presented at the 1st International Conference on Business, Strategy & Management, Kolkata, India. Retrieved from http://www.veloxian.com/ecj

Rodov, F., & Truong, S. (2015, April 2015). *Why schools should teach entrepreneurship.* Entrepreneurship Education. Retrieved from https://www.entrepreneur.com/article/245038

Senge, P. (2010). *The fifth discipline.* New York, NY: Doubleday.

Shane. S. A. (2009, November 16). Can academics be entrepreneurial? *New York Times.* Retrieved from https://boss.blogs.nytimes.com/2009/11/16/can-academics-be-entrepeneurial/?mcubz=1

Smith-Barrow, D. (2016, January 14). Find the right college to be an entrepreneur.

Retrieved from https://www.usnews.com/education/best-colleges/articles/2016-01-14/find-the-right-college-for-becoming-an-entrepreneur

Soundarajan, N., Camp, S. M., Lee, D., Ramnath, R., & Weide, B. W. (2016). NEWPATH: An innovative program to nurture IT entrepreneurs. *Advances in Engineering Education, 5*(1). Retrieved from http://files.eric.ed.gov/fulltext/EJ1090561.pdf

Tynan, K. (2015, November 23). Entrepreneurship, the new requirement in higher education. *MindBridge Partners.* Retrieved from http://edtechtimes.com/2015/11/23/entrepreneurship-the-new-requirement-in-higher-education/

Young, J. R. (2013, April 8). Social entrepreneurs bring new ideas, new conflicts to colleges. *The Chronicle of Higher Education.* Retrieved from http://www.chronicle.com/article/Social-Entrepreneurs-Bring/138365/

About the Authors...

Dr. Neil Mathur—picture and bio intentionally withheld for reasons of privacy.

 Dr. Cheryl A. Lentz affectionately known as *Doc C* to her students, is a university professor on faculty with Embry-Riddle University, Grand Canyon University (GCU), University of Phoenix, The University of the Rockies, and Walden University. Dr. Cheryl serves as a dissertation mentor / chair and committee member. She is also a dissertation coach, offering expertise as a professional editor for APA style for graduate thesis and doctoral dissertations, as well as faculty journal publications and books.

Awards include: Walden Faculty of the Year, DBA Program, 2016, UOP community service award, and 17 writing awards.

Dr. Cheryl is also an active member of Alpha Sigma Alpha Sorority.

She is a prolific author with more than 33 publications known for her writings on *The Golden Palace Theory of Management* and refractive thinking. Additional published works include her dissertation: *Strategic Decision Making in Organizational Performance, Journey Outside the Golden Palace, The Consumer Learner, Technology That Tutors, Effective Study Skills, The Dissertation Toolbox*, International Best Seller: *The Expert Success Solution*, and contributions to the award-winning series: *The Refractive Thinker®: Anthology of Doctoral Learners, Volumes I–XIII*.

To reach Dr. Cheryl Lentz for information on refractive thinking, professional editing, or guest speaking, please visit her websites: http://www.DrCherylLentz.com http://www.LentzLeadership.com or e-mail: drcheryllentz@gmail.com

Index

The Refractive Thinker®:
An Anthology of Higher Learning

The Refractive Thinker® Press

info@refractivethinker.com
www.RefractiveThinker.com
blog: www.DissertationPublishing.com

*Individual authors own the copyright to their individual materials.
The Refractive Thinker® Press has each author's permission to reprint.

Books are available through The Refractive Thinker® Press at special discounts for bulk purchases for the purpose of sales promotion, seminar attendance, or educational purposes. Special volumes can be created for specific purposes and to organizational specifications. Orders placed on www.RefractiveThinker.com for students and military receive a 15% discount. Please contact us for further details.

Refractive Thinker® logo by Joey Root; The Refractive Thinker® Press logo design by Jacqueline Teng, cover design by Peri Poloni-Gabriel, Knockout Design (knockoutbooks.com), cover design & production by Gary A. Rosenberg (thebookcouple.com).

I think therefore I am.
—RENEE DESCARTES

I critically think to be.
I refractively think to change the world.

THANK YOU FOR JOINING US as we continue to celebrate the accomplishments of doctoral scholars affiliated with many phenomenal institutions of higher learning. The purpose of the anthology series is to share a glimpse into the scholarly works of participating authors on various subjects.

The Refractive Thinker® serves the tenets of leadership, which is not simply a concept outside of the self, but comes from within, defining our very essence; where the search to define leadership becomes our personal journey, not yet a finite destination.

The Refractive Thinker® is an intimate expression of who we are: the ability to think beyond the traditional boundaries of thinking and critical thinking. Instead of mere reflection and evaluation, one challenges the very boundaries of the constructs itself. If thinking is *inside* the box, and critical thinking is *outside* the box, we add the next step of refractive thinking, *beyond* the box. Perhaps the need exists to dissolve the box completely. The authors within these pages are on a mission to change the world. They are never satisfied or quite content with *what is* or asking *why,* instead these authors intentionally strive to push and test the limits to ask *why not.*

We look forward to your interest in discussing future opportunities. Let our collection of authors continue the journey initiated with Volume I, to which *The Refractive Thinker®* will serve as our guide to future volumes. Come join us in our quest to be refractive thinkers and add your wisdom to the collective. We look forward to your stories.

Please contact The Refractive Thinker® Press for information regarding these authors and the works contained within these pages. Perhaps you or your organization may be looking for an author's expertise to incorporate as part of your annual corporate meetings as a keynote or guest speaker(s), perhaps to offer individual, or group seminars or coaching, or require their expertise as consultants.

Join us on our continuing adventures of *The Refractive Thinker*® where we expand the discussion specifically begun in Volume I: Leadership; Volume II (Editions 1–3): Research Methodology; Volume III: Change Management; Volume IV: Ethics, Leadership, and Globalization; Volume V: Strategy in Innovation; Volume VI: Post-Secondary Education; Volume VII: Social Responsibility; Volume VIII: Effective Business Practices in Motivation & Communication; Volume IX: Effective Business Practices in Leadership & Emerging Technologies; Volume X: Effective Business Strategies for the Defense Industry Sector; Volume XI: Women in Leadership; and Volume XII: Cybersecurity in an Increasingly Insecure World. All our volumes are themed to explore the realm of strategic thought, creativity, and innovation.

Dr. Cheryl A. Lentz, managing editor of The Lentz Leadership Institute, explains the unique benefits of the books for readers:

"They celebrate the diffusion of innovative refractive thinking through the writings of these doctoral scholars as they dare to think differently in search of new applications and understandings of research. Unlike most academic books that merely define research, The Refractive Thinker® offers unique applications of research from the perspective of multiple authors—each offering a chapter based on their specific expertise."

THE REFRACTIVE THINKER® PRESS

Volume I: An Anthology of Higher Learning

Volume II, 1st through 3rd Editions: Research Methodology

Volume III: Change Management

Volume IV: Ethics, Leadership, and Globalization

Volume V: Strategy in Innovation

Volume VI: Post-Secondary Education

Volume VII: Social Responsibility

Volume VIII: Effective Business Practices for Motivation and Communication

Volume IX: Effective Business Practices in Leadership & Emerging Technologies

Volume X: Effective Business Strategies for the Defense Industry Sector

Volume XI: Women in Leadership

Volume XII: Cybersecurity in an Increasingly Insecure World

Volume XIII: Entrepreneurship: Growing the Future of Business

Refractive Thinker volumes are available in e-book, Kindle®, iPad®, Nook®, and Sony Reader™, as well as individual e-chapters by author.

COMING SOON!
The Refractive Thinker®: Volume XIV: Health Care

Telephone orders: Call us at 702.719.9214

Email Orders: drcheryllentz@gmail.com

Website orders: Please place orders through our website:
www.RefractiveThinker.com

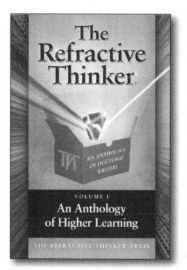

The Refractive Thinker®: Volume I:
An Anthology of Higher Learning

The title of this book, *The Refractive Thinker®*, was chosen intentionally to highlight the ability of these doctoral scholars to bend thought, to converge its very essence on the ability to obliquely pass through the perspective of another. The goal is to ask and ponder the right questions; to dare to think differently, to find new applications within unique and cutting-edge dimensions, ultimately to lead where others may follow or to risk forging perhaps an entirely new path.

The Refractive Thinker®: Volume II:
Research Methodology

The authors within these pages are on a mission to change the world, never satisfied or quite content with what is or asking *why,* instead these authors intentionally strive to push and test the limits to ask *why not. The Refractive Thinker®* is an intimate expression of who we are—the ability to think beyond the traditional boundaries of thinking and critical thinking. Instead of mere reflection and evaluation, one challenges the very boundaries of the constructs itself.

For more information, please visit our website: www.RefractiveThinker.com

The Refractive Thinker®: Volume II: Research Methodology, 2nd Edition

As in Volume I, the authors within these pages are on a mission to change the world, never satisfied or quite content with what is or asking *why*, instead these authors intentionally strive to push and test the limits to ask *why not. The Refractive Thinker®* is an intimate expression of who we are—the ability to think beyond the traditional boundaries of thinking and critical thinking. Instead of mere reflection and evaluation, one challenges the very boundaries of the constructs itself.

*Chosen as Finalist, Education/Academic category
The USA "Best Books 2011" Awards,
sponsored by USA Book News*

The Refractive Thinker®: Volume II: Research Methodology, 3rd Edition

If thinking is inside the box, and critical thinking is outside the box, refractive thinking is beyond the box. The Refractive Thinker® series provides doctoral scholars with a collaborative opportunity to promote and publish their work in a peer reviewed publication. Our goal is to provide an affordable outlet for scholars that supports the tremendous need for dynamic dialogue and innovation while providing clout and recognition for each.

Winner in the 2013 Global Ebook "Non-Fiction Anthology" category; Finalist, the USA "Best Books 2013" Award; and eLit Bronze 2014 winner

For more information, please visit our website: www.RefractiveThinker.com

The Refractive Thinker®: Volume III: Change Management

This next offering in the series shares yet another glimpse into the scholarly works of these authors, specifically on the topic of change management. In addition to exploring various aspects of change management, the purpose of *The Refractive Thinker®* is also to serve the tenets of leadership. Leadership is not simply a concept outside of the self, but comes from within, defining our very essence; where the search to define leadership becomes our personal journey, not yet a finite destination.

The Refractive Thinker®: Volume IV: Ethics, Leadership, and Globalization

The purpose of this volume is to highlight the scholarly works of these authors on the topics of ethics, leadership, and concerns within the global landscape of business. Join us as we venture forward to showcase the authors of Volume IV, and continue to celebrate the accomplishments of these doctoral scholars affiliated with many phenomenal institutions of higher learning.

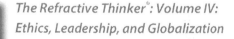

For more information, please visit our website: www.RefractiveThinker.com

The Refractive Thinker Press Wins 2011 eLit Award for Digital Publishing Excellence

The Refractive Thinker: Vol. V: Strategy in Innovation has been named the winner of the Gold in the Anthology category of the 2011 eLit Awards!

The Refractive Thinker®: Volume VI: Post-Secondary Education

Celebrate the diffusion of innovative refractive thinking through the writings of these doctoral scholars as they dare to think differently in search of new applications and understandings of post-secondary education. Unlike most academic books that merely define research, *The Refractive Thinker®* offers commentary regarding the state of post-secondary education from the perspective of multiple authors—each offering a chapter based on their specific expertise.

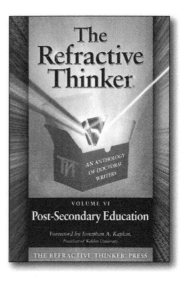

For more information, please visit our website: www.RefractiveThinker.com

The Refractive Thinker®:
Volume VII: Social Responsibility

The Refractive Thinker® Volume VII, is available to scholars and researchers. The book is part of the multiple award-winning REFRACTIVE THINKER® series published by The Refractive Thinker® Press.

Finalist in the "Anthologies: Non-Fiction" category of the 2013 International Book Awards!

Winner in the "Education/Academic" category, The USA Best Books 2012 Awards, sponsored by USA Book News

The Refractive Thinker®: Volume VIII: Effective Practices for Motivation and Communication

The Spring 2014 release of the Refractive Thinker® anthology marks a new direction for the publication. While previous editions have been curated from a purely academic standpoint, Volume VIII makes the real world connection by bridging the gap. Academicians identify and address the issues in each chapter and Dr. Cheryl Lentz, The Academic Entrepreneur™, provides an interpretation for application into today's business world.

This volume is a true bridge between scholarship and the business community.

Finalist in the 2014 USA Best Book Awards in the "Education/Academic" category.
2015 Next Generation Indie Book Awards Finalist

For more information, please visit our website: www.RefractiveThinker.com

The Refractive Thinker®: Volume IX:
Effective Business Practices
in Leadership & Emerging Technologies

The Refractive Thinker® Volume IX, is available to scholars and researchers. While previous editions have been curated from a purely academic standpoint, Volume IX continues building on the real world connection by bridging the gap. Academicians identify and address the issues in each chapter and provide an interpretation for application into today's business world.

Digital Only: $9.95. Under Business & Economics/Leadership publications.

The Refractive Thinker®: Volume X:
Effective Business Strategies
for the Defense Industry Sector

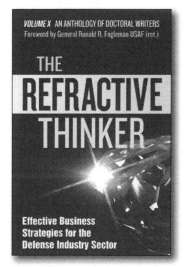

Join **General Ronald R. Fogleman** and contributing scholars as they discuss research regarding effective business strategies for the defense sector. The conversations include discussions regarding the struggles of a nation to define the way forward regarding the impacts of Defense procurement, Defense health care spending, economic impacts on veteran owned businesses and succession planning, solutions to manage and lead disasters, economic challenges, reduction of energy costs, and exploration of leadership strategies to drive business practices important to the future of our nation. The goal is this volume is to find innovative solutions for more effective outcomes to drive change.

For more information, please visit our website: www.RefractiveThinker.com

The Refractive Thinker®: Volume XI:
Women in Leadership

Sally Helgesen and contributing scholars discuss research that will influence how women's leadership is understood and supported in the years ahead. They also offer fresh insights into mentoring and coaching practices, the impact of continued shifts in demographics, and the role of women in specific cultures in articulating

a sustainable vision of the future. Such contributions will expand and enrich the programmatic offerings that help speed women on their leadership journeys into the future.

Digital Only: $9.95. Under Business & Economics/Leadership publications.

The Refractive Thinker®: Volume XII:
Cybersecurity in an Increasingly
Insecure World

Join contributing scholars as they discuss current research regarding the challenges of the world of cybersecurity and its effects in and on the marketplace. This volume contains research shaping the conversation regarding what the future may hold to protect businesses and consumers regarding the perils of digital technology.

For more information, please visit our website: www.RefractiveThinker.com

The Dissertation Toolbox

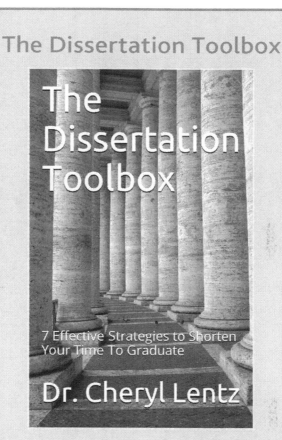

Struggling to complete your doctoral journey? Having trouble writing your dissertation or your doc study? Help is on the way! Join Dr. Cheryl Lentz— 16-time award-winning author and Walden University Faculty of the Year in 2016—in her new book to help you shorten your time to graduation with proven and effective strategies. Save time and money learning to create systems to help move you forward through the process more quickly.

With Foreword by Dr. Julie Ducharme, Preface by Dr. Gillian Silver, and contributions from publishing intern Josue Villanueva.

www.ThePensieroPress.com

So You Think You Can Edit?
9 Self-Editing Tips for the Novice and Experienced Writer

So You Think You Can Edit? is Dr. Cheryl's most recent book that speaks to the precision of competent writing and editing. She underscores a myriad of practical techniques for validating our choices so we may refine our personal writing acumen, rather than relying on editors to carry the weight. Further, she makes a legitimate case for considering the impressions made when we speak through our articulation and review choices. Each of us, doctorate learner and business executive alike, stands to gain from her insightful guidance.

The Expert Success Solution
Chapter 5—What Would Einstein Do?

Join Dr. Cheryl as she offers proven strategies to shorten your learning curve to think beyond limits when facing problems in your personal and professional settings. Learn to fail faster to succeed sooner using proven skills to move you forward more effectively through individual coaching, Tele Seminars, and online classes using The WRIST Method. Remember, the helping hand you need is at the end of your W-R-I-S-T!

www.ThinkingBeyondLimits.com

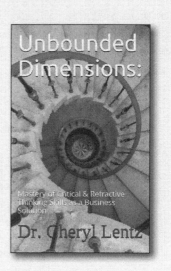

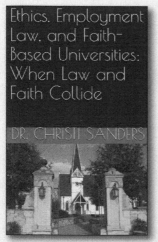

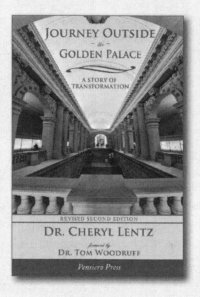

TECHNOLOGY THAT TUTORS:
7 Ways to Save Time by Using the Blog as a Teaching Tool

University professors seem to have the same conversation with different students time after time. What if we could be available to our students whenever and wherever we're needed, virtually?

Technology offers such a solution with the creation of the blog. Think of it as technology that tutors 24/7. Welcome to the world of the blog where some of our efforts as professors are now scalable. Learn how you can create a video (with transcript), embed it on your blog, and simply provide the link to your students as the need or topic may arise in class discussions.

Please join me on this journey as I offer a path to shorten your learning curve with increased efficiency in teaching methods as we look to the blog with seven ways to save time by using the blog as a teaching tool.   Visit **www.TechnologyThatTutors.com**.

WELCOME HOME:
Siberian Husky Rescue Handbook
11 Tips to Welcome a Siberian Rescue into Your Family

Welcome to the Siberian Husky Rescue of New Mexico, Inc. Handbook for new Siberian owners.

Our goal for creating this book is to help new owners prepare themselves for welcoming their newest Siberian Husky rescue into their home. Making a decision to rescue can be one of the most rewarding decisions of a family IF everyone is well prepared. Proceeds benefit this 501c3 rescue group.

This book is written by Dr. Cheryl Lentz, the founder of Siberian Husky Rescue of New Mexico, International Best Selling Author, Speaker, and Professor.

Visit **www.DrCherylLentz.com/Siberian-Husky-Rescue**

PUBLICATIONS ORDER FORM

Please send the following books from The Refractive Thinker®:

❏ *Volume I: An Anthology of Higher Learning*
❏ *Volume II: Research Methodology*
❏ *Volume II: Research Methodology, 2nd Edition*
❏ *Volume II: Research Methodology, 3rd Edition*
❏ *Volume III: Change Management*
❏ *Volume IV: Ethics, Leadership, and Globalization*
❏ *Volume V: Strategy in Innovation*
❏ *Volume VI: Post-Secondary Education*
❏ *Volume VII: Social Responsibility*
❏ *Volume VIII: Effective Business Practices*
❏ *Volume IX: Effective Business Practices in Leadership & Emerging Technologies*
❏ *Volume X: Effective Business Strategies for the Defense Industry Sector*
❏ *Volume XI: Women in Leadership*
❏ *Volume XII: Cybersecurity*
❏ *Volume XIII: Entrepreneurship*

Please contact the Refractive Thinker® Press for book prices, e-book prices, and shipping. Individual e-chapters available by author: $3.95 (plus applicable tax). www.RefractiveThinker.com

❏ *So You Think You Can Edit?*
❏ *The Expert Success Solution*
❏ *The Unbounded Dimensions Series*
❏ *Ethics, Employment Law, and Faith-Based Universities*
❏ *Effective Study Skills in 5 Simple Steps*

❏ *Technology That Tutors*
❏ *Siberian Husky Rescue*
❏ *The Consumer Learner*
❏ *Journey Outside the Golden Palace*
❏ *The Dissertation Toolbox*

Please send more FREE information:
❏ Speaking engagements   ❏ Educational seminars   ❏ Consulting

Join our mailing list:

Name: _____

Address: _____

City: _____   State: _____   Zip: _____

Telephone: _____   Email: _____

See our website for shipping rates.

E-mail form to: The Refractive Thinker® Press/Pensiero Press
             drcheryllentz@gmail.com

Yes, I would like to participate in:

❏ **Doctoral Volume**(s) for a specific university or organization:

Name: _____

Contact Person: _____

Telephone: _____ E-mail: _____

❏ **Specialized Volume**(s) Business or Themed:

Name: _____

Contact Person: _____

Telephone: _____ E-mail: _____

E-mail form to: The Refractive Thinker® Press
drcheryllentz@gmail.com
www.RefractiveThinker.com

Made in the USA
San Bernardino, CA
26 November 2017